BIRTH *of a* Jewel

Stories of Wisdom and Inspiration

TERESE NEELY POTTINGER

First Edition

PAGE PUBLISHING
Conneaut Lake, PA

First originally published by Page Publishing 2023

ISBN 979-8-89157-916-3 (pbk)
ISBN 979-8-88960-922-3 (hc)
ISBN 979-8-88960-908-7 (digital)

Printed in the United States of America

CONTENTS

FOREWORD

I have always imagined that paradise will be a kind of library.

—Luis Borgas

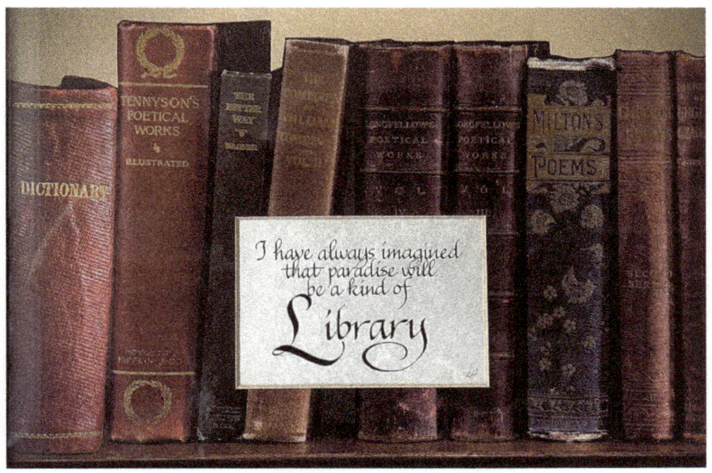

Credit of Photo Linda Harris

Books have been in my life for as long as I can remember.

As a small girl in the midsixties, we had a Bookmobile (it was a bus turned into a mobile library), which came to the neighborhood every two weeks at our grocery store up the street. To receive a library card back then, you just had to know how to spell your full name, and I was excited when I heard this at five-and-a-half years old. So I practiced writing my name until it was perfect. And then, I proudly stepped into the Bookmobile, wrote my name slowly and neatly on a brand-new card, and received the best gift ever.

Even though I was young, I was allowed to go on my own. I would sit on the curb, rereading the books I was to exchange for new ones. Seeing the bus enter the lot was so thrilling that I would stand right up, books under my arm, and start waving. It felt like Santa was coming to see me personally, and I could not wait!

When the doors swung open and I stepped up the stairs, it made my heart jump to breathe in the smell of all these books. When I came home, I'd go straight to my bedroom and put them under my bed so I could start reading before I went to bed and as soon as I opened my eyes in the morning. Gosh, if young kids were allowed to drink coffee, it would have made the moment complete.

After I retired, I wanted to work part-time doing something interesting and enjoyable. And when it was time to go home, work was done! This concept was unheard of before my husband and I moved to a small rural community where a little library stood out from the Civil War battlefields and was only five minutes from our house. The first time I passed by, I loudly said, "Oh, a library! I want to work there!" I had never worked at one, but I was up for the challenge. Surprisingly enough, they had an opening, and when I said I had never worked at a library, they still hired me—definitely a God-wink moment.

On the first day of work, I walked through those doors, took a deep breath, and thought I had died and gone to heaven.

The first week I shadowed my coworkers to learn the ropes. People came in asking for all kinds of books, and they were able to direct and give recommendations for what everyone was looking for. Naturally, I was concerned because most books I read were nonfiction and didn't know many authors' names.

I remember coming home feeling a bit troubled.

The positive outlook I've carried all my life woke up with me the next morning. So I decided when I was at work, I'd randomly pick a book and an audiobook from different genres to read and get to know the authors' names. Sometimes, I would walk down an aisle, not look at any of the books, and feel the cover or open my hand wide with eyes closed, feeling which one might be calling me to read. Other times, I'd go to the biographies section and take one without looking and do the same in the young adult section.

It worked!

Six months later, I was reading three books a week, one in the morning with a spiritual vibe, an exciting novel in the afternoon, and a quiet, reflective one before bed. I listened to the audiobooks when I'd go to the main store, which was thirty minutes away and when we traveled.

By nine months, when someone stopped by the desk asking what an interesting book would be to take on a long drive, something they wanted to learn about, or just about anything, I was their go-to person!

Yep, I felt like the library, and I were merging quite nicely.

Sometimes, a person would walk up to the desk, smack a book down on the counter, and say, "This was an incredible book. You should read it!"

I'd look quizzically at them and say, "Tell me why you think I would like it."

As they explained the ins and outs of the book without giving too much away, I could see through their eyes they were living in the story as they spoke with such delight that I wanted to feel that experience of the book too.

"Sold!" I said. "Next time you're in, ask me what I thought." They'd leave happy that someone was going to read a book that they thought was fantastic.

But if we think about it, aren't we the same way?

When we moved a few years later to the city, I worked as a librarian assistant and continued to read and experience the rich and exciting world of stories. I grew leaps and bounds in life and the inner changes I made through reading.

During those eight years, I lost count of how many books I read, and there were times I'd wake up, look at the huge stack on the nightstand, and tell myself I would not bring any more books home until I read all these.

Sure enough, I'd come home with at least two more that day, thinking, *Could I be addicted to books?* As I pondered this, it gave way to a scary but exciting thought: *Wow, that would be so cool! What a great thing to be addicted too!*

During my years at the library, I connected with everything. Weirdly, I felt I had become the library. (Those who love books and find a kinship with libraries will understand that comment.)

I'd watch people when there were slower moments at the front desk. Some were lost in the pages of their books, some were taking notes, and some were reading to their small children whose sweet faces were mesmerized by the pictures.

I'd fantasize that maybe one day after I'm long gone, my life may become a book, and someone will pull it out of a shelf and take it home. Then, hopefully, they'll find it an excellent read.

And here I am.

I am not long gone and am excited to share the wisdom I have found in the life lessons I have accumulated through the experiences of my sixty-plus years walking on this earth. Some of the stories may have you laughing; some may stop you in your tracks, and the tears will flow; then others may leave you pondering about your own journey and the lessons you can share.

I have always believed there are no coincidences and the choices we make (as in picking up this book) are made to bring an experience into our lives. These times can guide us to expand, grow, and learn more about ourselves as we move forward.

Thank you for pulling this book off a shelf in a library, store, or online. You have supported my dream of shining my light so others may find their path just by how I live my life. I am honored and in gratitude. Thank you.

I am a writer and reader on Medium (https://medium.com).

Medium is a social publishing platform that
is open to all and home to a diverse array of sto-

> ries, ideas, and perspectives. Anyone can be an individual contributor, and popular topics range from mental health to social media, and from world affairs and trending news to productivity hacks. (August 7, 2021)

I feel hope, incredible joy, and encouragement when reading articles, stories, and poetry from our creative younger writers. They take my breath away often, and it seems just about every piece they post pulls us internally for lessons we seek for growth, improvement, and the clarity to reinvent our very being. The jewels found through their writings are stepping stones to create the very essence of our lives. When it is time for me to pass the torch, I will feel no worries whatsoever knowing the world will be in good and safe hands.

If Medium feels like a venue you would be interested in exploring, you won't be disappointed. While there, take a look at my platform where you will find more of my stories like the ones you will be reading here, including an option to listen to me read them. I would love to see you there!

Note from the author: When it comes to God, we all have our unique expression of the name we choose that brings the most comfort to us. Throughout this book, I refer to God as Spirit, our Creator, and All That Is.

ACKNOWLEDGMENTS

If I could have chosen a first and middle name for myself before I was born, it would have been Grace and Gratitude. The definition of *Grace* is the influence or Spirit of God operating in humans to regenerate or strengthen them, while *Gratitude* is the quality or feeling of being grateful or thankful.

Both represent the very being that I am. This didn't come to fruition until I learned through many teachers how Spirit has infinite Grace to share with all of us and Its Gratitude for each of us is just as endless. My world changed realizing this, and I was then able to live from the place where Spirit and I live as one.

This book and its stories all come from the same place where Spirit lives and moves through me, and I am in gratitude.

To my mother and my father, you were the yin and yang, the light and dark of my upbringing. Without you, I would not have become the unique jewel I believe myself to be. In recognition of this truth, the honor and love I carry for you both is unconditional. Thank you for giving me life.

I would like to sincerely thank my husband, Jeff, for his constant support, guidance, editing, and lending a patient ear, for without him, this book would have been more than challenging to publish. And for carrying my heart through some of the indecisiveness and the feelings of not being courageous enough to write the book that has been calling me from within all along. I love you forever and a day.

To my siblings, Mike, Kathy, Patty, Laurie, and Randy, when I think of us and all we have gone through together, this quote from Sandman Saha comes to heart: "The greatest gift our parents gave us was each other." It is genuine and priceless. Thank you for your support and love throughout my life.

To my children, Bobby, Johnny, David and Joseph. Each of you has your own stories in your upbringing together and apart. I have observed how your lives have unfolded into the extraordinary adults you have become because of those complex, sorrowful, and joyous experiences. The growth I have attained and the wisdom I have encountered by who you are individually and together have given me the gift of profound joy. Because of this, it has brought me to the pages of this book in admiration for the awareness of what love can do when it chooses to learn from those experiences and be the teacher for those of us still wandering for direction.

I know you must walk your own path, but rest assured that my love will always surround you in the light for guidance when needed. Thank you for loving me unconditionally. I love you as I breathe.

To our blended family of eleven children and sixteen grandchildren. You have renewed my faith in humanity. And when it is my time to pass the baton, I know beyond a shadow of a doubt this world will be a healthier and happier place to live because of you. Keep living your best life now.

To my Medium family, the responses you have left on my writing platform have continuously given me the validation that I am indeed a writer. And I can honestly say that because of your stories, poems, breathtaking photos, and humor, the growth I have accumulated had skyrocketed from where I was when I joined this unique website. I thank all of you for the experience of you!

And last but most profoundly, Jeshua. From the moment I opened my heart to our connection, our kinship, the world made sense. The guidance and wisdom of your teachings change my life by how you lived yours on earth. I am forever grateful and at peace.

Photo by MMcKein / pixabay.com

1

Love and Fear

The Mystery of Human Existence Lies Not In Just Staying Alive, But In Finding Something To Live For.

—Fyodor Dostoyevsky

There are only two kinds of energy in the world: love and fear. Everything stems from either one, like branches on the trees that flow up and out and never cease. Both drive people to do either fantastic, incredible things or despicable, horrible things. We choose in every moment, unconsciously or consciously, to do one or the other. It is seen in every corner of the world and has been going on since the beginning of time.

Fear and I have held hands for most of my life. There were moments when fear pinned me to the ground and movement was not an option, and all I could do was allow it to engulf me. And then there were times I backed it up and dared it to give me its best shot. I am not new to this world, and to surprise me with what people can do to themselves and each other is not easy.

Compassion, forgiveness, and understanding of how others tick, including myself, are crucial to my existence.

Even though sorrow is not far behind, I decide to pull the positive out of every fearful, hateful story that passes through my vision. I also choose to praise and be grateful for every beautiful, loving story that passes through my heart.

I no longer downgrade who I am or call myself names that I would never call anyone else.

In conversations with people, I don't join in with the negativity and redirect the words toward a more positive outlook. And at times, it is received with annoying glances and rolls of the eyes, as if saying, "Here she goes again."

Because of this, I have been told more than I can count that I have my head in the clouds or I've gotten lost in La La land and that I am too passive or positive and not grounded because of not reacting to difficult news in this world like others think I should. But we all have our way of experiencing life.

I have made many mistakes in my life, but I've come to respect those mistakes as learning tools for growth and expansion. I am a good person, and my center has always been with Spirit by my side, taking It on my healthy and unhealthy paths. As two of my closest friends have told me, I would not be the person I am today if I had not gone through these experiences.

I love the person I am today, the heart that I am, and to deny respect for this truth is denying the beautiful creation Spirit created, even at my most destructive times as a human. When Spirit is ALL Love, ALL understanding, and ALL knowing, how can It look at us any different? It is us who put restrictions on loving ourselves and others.

I have been honored to love so many hearts in my life and to now share the last twenty-two years with not only an excellent teacher but with someone who has the rare gift of not needing me, and for that, I have been able to explore different avenues and paths this world has to offer for my personal growth, alone and together.

As sure as the sun is shining through my window and onto this page right now, there is a deep knowing that I am here for a purpose: *YOU* and the experiences of *US*.

Thoughts to ponder:

What is it that you live for? What purpose do you carry that moves you to step forward in making a difference within yourself and perhaps others?

2

The Birth of a Jewel

Credit / Courtesy of pixabay.com

Learn to light a candle in the darkest of someone's life. Be the light that helps others see; it is what gives life its deepest significance.

—Roy T. Bennett

Visualize the mind of Spirit, and take a ride into my heart. If there is a quiet movement of your own heart as you read, fasten your seatbelt because maybe, somewhere within, there is an awakening to a remembrance of your unique relationship with *ALL THAT IS*.

A space seeped into the great mind of our Creator—that space was me.

Spirit is suddenly aware of this space and instantly falls in love and decides to create this mesmerizing love feeling into a beautiful one-of-a-kind jewel. As It holds the treasure up and into Its Light, the facets shine like nothing It has ever seen.

It has an *ah-ha* moment and comes up with a whimsical idea! The universe shakes as Spirit says with joy: "I will put this perfect, magnificent jewel on Earth, and it will represent me. I shall also give it a glorious purpose to live by. The light it carries is so brilliant that wherever it goes and whatever it does, it will shine so bright that others will easily find their path. It will also walk on the Earth as the presence of love, singing, dancing, and creating a beautiful world around itself, even amid the fear of confusion and disruption. No matter what difficulties it goes through, it will always choose to shine its light and always choose love over hate, kindness over meanness, and bring comfort and joy to those who seek it. It will be my protégé and I its faithful guide. The deep stillness of Me that lives within each soul will be felt in its most fearful moments, and the reminder of *where* it was created will awaken in peace and reassurance."

Upon hearing this, the jewel's light expanded in joy and deep awe. In trusting these words, it was ready to be sent down to Earth and begin a journey of a lifetime.

Spirit leans Its head back, releasing a deep, heartfelt, warm chuckle while bringing this love jewel to Its lips. Then, kissing It softly, It quietly says, "Are you ready, my delightful creation?"

With the rainbow colors of the facets glowing with excitement, it replies, "I Am!"

Spirit smiles and says, "Yes, you are! And I applaud your awareness of this." Its lights blink, and Spirit added, "I created you, in that which is ALL LOVE. So YOU are THAT I AM." This little jewel blushed, and Its heart expanded tenfold.

And with that, Spirit took a deep smooth breath and blew the jewel gracefully to Earth like a feather falling from an eagle's wing flowing down through the clouds. As it shifted into the atmosphere of what would become this little miracle's home for a short time, it knew it would be spreading its Creator's love and breathed in joy, gratitude, and captivating anticipation.

And so, It is.

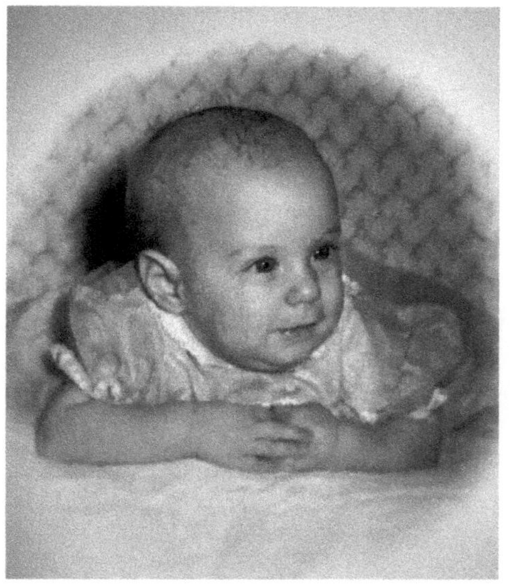

The reflection in my eyes even at this young age shows a calm joy. The adult me, now, rests in this natural wisdom.

Thought to ponder:

It is said that Spirit flows through everything and everyone. When we're open and allow it, we can see this everywhere. Where does Spirit flow in your life?

3

A Moment of Recognition

Credit / Photo by author

Spirit,
This is such an important time in my life.
You have been silent but ever so close.
I see you as I look out to the sparkling water.
I taste you in the watermelon I let
        dissolve in my mouth.

And in that first sip of tea.
I hear you in the voice of the birds,
And the beautiful music I listen to.
I can touch you when I wipe a
    tear from my cheek,
And feel you as I meditate through
    every vein in my body.

Thank you for loving me, for
    watching out for me,
and listening to my deepest desires, for
    I am living those dreams now.
And for helping me persevere at loving myself,
when my ego tries to beat that love
    up with guilts of my past.

Please continue holding my hand and guiding
    me to understand my true self,
the place where you and I are one.
Where love is the foundation,
    and my soul is hungry
to experience the treasures of your
    connection with me.

I believe and trust that you will take
    good care as we journey,
and will open my eyes even wider to understand
how important it is to love myself
    as you love me.

And so it is.

Thought to ponder:

How do you love yourself, and what place of honor do you have where you and Spirit become one?

4

"And We Begin Again"

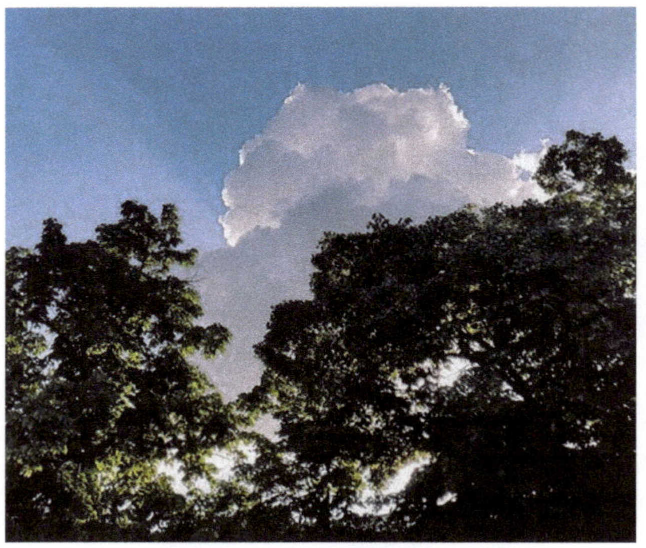

DiDs / Pexel.com

I use an app called Insight Timer. People worldwide participate in the music, classes, and meditations this app has to offer. I have become friends with a few of them. I have enjoyed one in particular, Willowrose, as she calls herself, and once, after thanking her for meditating with me, she responded, "…and we begin again."

The phrase struck a spark in me. It was simple and felt very freeing just saying it. Afterward, when I stepped out for my morning walk, I took a deep breath and said, "And we begin again."

As I walked, I was curious, *Why didn't Willowrose say, "And I begin again?"*

Oh, she meant she and I begin again—*We* got it!

I reflected on this.

The *we* could be another person and me.

The *we* could be me, as a human and my soul.

The *we* could be Spirit and me.

The *we* could just be me and the world that begins again.

Nice, I have options.

After weighing all those options, I have decided that the *we* will be whomever I feel at the time is essential to join me.

So I began to think about other questions I could use "And we begin again." For example: As you lie down to sleep, do you ever wish you could erase the day and have a do-over? Have you ever said something to someone you regretted, wishing you could delete the whole conversation like it never happened? Have you ever been with a group of people and didn't feel like you fit in? Have you been in a room full of surface-only conversations and just wanted to excuse yourself because that way of communicating doesn't work for you anymore? Have there been times when you felt a deep void and didn't have a clue how to fill it or where it even was? Have you ever put your feet on the floor upon waking and wondered what kind of day it would be and were unsure if you were ready?

As I get older, these questions float around in my mind. We have been taught to seek answers so we can feel better. Sometimes, I find answers; other times, I don't.

Do we always need answers? I don't think so. So we can sit in these questions and listen for the answers or feel the peace in the questions themselves.

With many of the questions above, I now use "And we begin again" and feel comfortably aligned without knowing answers or wanting any. What's nice is when using this phrase *we* is always with me and I am never alone.

"And we begin again" is the perfect phrase to bring freshness to any do-over, regret, frustration, or question as we start each day.

Thought to ponder:
Where in your life could you begin again?

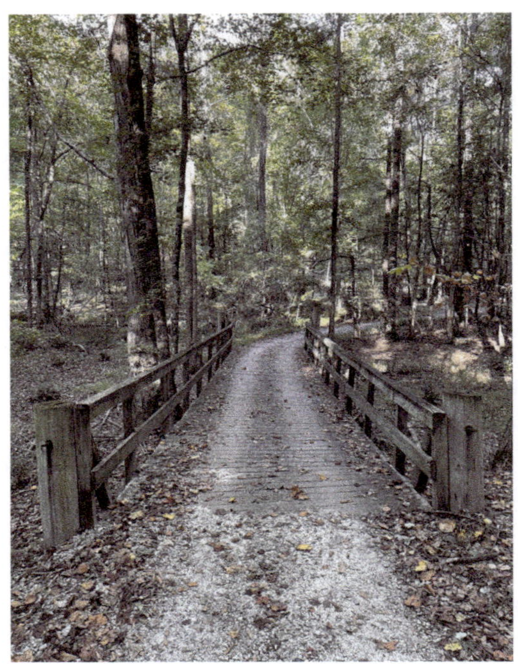

Photo taken by author

5

Cancer: A Positive Teacher

Photo by Christopher Campbell on Unsplash

The word *cancer* has a frightening effect on people, and I was no different when the doctor told me I had breast cancer. I was only twenty-nine when they said it had been growing inside me for five years. It felt like I'd been taken from a relaxing soak in a hot tub and dunked in freezing water!

I knew that I could react to this disrupting news in either a positive or negative way. I could become full of despair about the unfair hand I had been dealt, which would only make life miserable for my children and certainly would not teach them how to handle their own challenges, or decide to learn all that I could about this disease and accept that I did have cancer but not allow it to dominate my every thought and action. I chose the latter approach because my spirit would not allow me to let cancer "swallow me up," and once I came to terms with my situation, my life took on new meaning. I decided that I would never blame Spirit for this disease and find out as much as I could to help understand what was going on inside of me. I read books and spoke with women who had already gone through this experience, and most importantly, I was determined to take the time to look at all the good things and people in my life.

And I did. I had been diagnosed right before Mother's Day and thought it would be a perfect time to write my mother a gratitude letter. I told her that no matter the outcome of this disease, I was forever grateful that she gave me life. I thanked her for how she loved me and teaching me the importance of loving Spirit and myself. I took the time to study a flower and watch insects feel their way around the earth. I would stop and watch birds and butterflies fly with such freedom. I'd focused on my boys' laughter and would hold them for hours while they slept.

When it came time for me to leave for the hospital, I was ready. I felt that life had been very good to me, and I was thankful. Whatever the outcome, I trusted Spirit to take care of me. I did not pray that I would be healed—that was a given, so instead, I prayed for the strength to handle the outcome with dignity and peace.

Tears flooded my eyes when the doctor told me three days after the surgery that the cancer was not found in the thirteen lymph nodes that were removed.

Sitting with the doctor a few weeks later, he said that because cancer had been growing inside my body for five years, he strongly advised me to start with radiation and chemo treatments right away. I declined.

Back in the eighties, I saw women my age dying, even with both treatments, so after deep reflection, I didn't feel it was for me. My doctor then gave me another option. Due to my age, the researchers wanted to follow me throughout my life and, at times, would give me a placebo or a drug for testing purposes. I thanked him but passed on the invitation. He was a very kind man, and when we said goodbye, there was sadness in his eyes, which meant he did not think I was going to be alive much longer.

As I walked down a hospital hall ten years later, visiting a friend, we bumped into each other. He recognized me right away, stopped, and looked stunned. I smiled, hugged him, and said, "Doctor, you're looking at me like I'm a ghost!"

And the response was, "I think I have. You are well?"

I smiled even more significantly and said, "Yes, very well. Thank you!"

Even though testing must be yearly, I felt I have another chance to love life, watch my children grow, and help others find the positive even in the most fearful of times.

Cancer has taught me that one day you are here and then next you may not, that I need to embrace each day no matter what goes on and to realize that each experience has something to teach me for growth and wisdom, which goes hand and hand at times with pain and heartache, and most importantly, not to take anyone or any experience for granted as I journey.

I am now sixty-plus years young and still loving life one day at a time and shining my light so others find their path.

Thought to ponder:

What experiences have you been through that challenged you to go deep and pull up the strength and courage to come to life differently?

6

Giving and Receiving: Finding the Balance

Photo by Pascal Bernardon on Unsplash

We must first learn how to receive from the heart in order to give from the heart.

At one point in my life, I was a single mom raising two boys. We didn't have much, and I worked two jobs, but we managed.

In the beginning, I was making below-poverty level. Food and furnishings were scarce, but with the generosity of many friends and family, we were taken care of in the kindest of ways.

At first, it was a struggle for me to receive their help, but seeing the joy on their faces brought me to a place of acceptance. When I offered to pay them back as soon as possible, they replied, "No need, just pay it forward when the opportunity presents itself." The words resonated with me, so I decided to carry them in my heart to remember for the rest of my life.

At the same time, my mom lived about forty-five minutes away. She was not in good health, so I cleaned her house, bought groceries, and cared for her needs every week. Mom appreciated my visits, but I could tell she had a tough time receiving the help too. I then reminded her of all the years she had taken care of us five kids and worked full-time; giving back to her was an honor.

Moving forward as life does, it was a hectic time. I worked a full-time job during the day and ran our church's Youth Group in the evenings and most weekends. I shared with a very close friend that I didn't know how I was going to get everything done for an upcoming retreat.

She smiled and said, "Give me some of the work. I have the time, and I'd like to help out."

I quickly replied, "Thank you, but you've got a family to take care of too. I'll figure it out."

She was quiet for a moment, looked at me, and said, "You know, Terry, you can really be selfish."

I was startled by her comment and gasped, "How can you say that? You know I'd give anyone the shirt off my back."

She replied, "Yes, I know, and how does that make you feel?"

I exclaimed. "Amazing! My heart rises. I feel valued and living my purpose."

My wise friend then responded, "Then, why don't you let others experience those same feelings by allowing them to help you?"

Whoa, that was a deer in the headlight moment! Her words were so wise, so simple, and so accurate!

When we are open to receiving without guilt, without feeling we owe something, and are receiving with gratitude from a giving heart, the energy is the same.

Giving from the heart makes us feel warm, connected, and valued.

Receiving from the heart allows us to learn that honest gratitude provides the other with the same warmth and sincere feeling inside their heart.

I have always believed there is a balance within us, just waiting to be put back into place when life gets wonky. Too much of anything can throw us off, like being on a teeter-totter. Put too much weight on one side, and we get stuck. Put too much force into pushing back up, and we throw the other rider off. Find the right balance between the two, and we both enjoy the ride!

Thought to ponder:

Find your balance between giving and receiving, and you may just enjoy life's ride so much more!

Credit / EvertonVila / unsplash.com

7

Letting Go

If It's Out of Your Hands, It Deserves the Freedom to Be Out of Your Mind Too

—Ivan Nuru

Photo by Austin Kehmeier on Unsplash

If the problems of your world, country, state, city, friends, neighbors, parents, adult children, and siblings are out of your hands, it is essential to let them slip through your fingers like water.

Not to say, if you have the justified call, the means, and the deep-seated pull to help, then lead the camel to water to help take a sip or two of that refreshing healing liquid. This way, they can experience the awakening of their senses to move forward.

If they insist on keeping their mouths open, grasping our hands tight for more, and we do, we are not helping. Instead, we are teaching them how not to learn for themselves, how not to walk on their own two feet, and how not to build their own grounding space on this earth.

When this interaction continues, our strength will eventually diminish as if we were a balloon when the knot is released. When the ones riding on our backs see that we are no longer capable of carrying them, they will climb off, move away, and find someone else.

When we take over the responsibilities of the choices others make in their life, it is not teaching; it only depletes.

Many of us will take the "easy way out" when offered. Why? Because it *is* easy. But most times, easy is not a great learning tool for growth.

As we share our experiences with others and live by example, we become true teachers.

When we genuinely realize a situation is not in our hands, it will give way to allowing that situation and outcome to be free to roam anywhere except in our minds. We tend to keep worries locked inside the mind as a consolation prize for not stepping in to fix the problems that are not ours. "Okay, if I can't improve this problem or fix it, I'll just think about it 24/7 and worry about the outcome."

Giving our energy to constant worrying leaves no space in our minds to enjoy the freedom we deserve as human beings to create, explore, and grow.

When I first read this quote, it took some time to fully understand what "It deserves the freedom to be out of your mind too" meant. I kept picturing this concerned energy bouncing off the walls of my brain, trying to move out but couldn't.

I was giving myself such a headache.

But once I realized I was holding it tightly in, it helped tremendously in moments of frustration, anger, and fear of having to let go of what was not mine. It has lifted and lightened my heart, and the heaviness I'd carried surrounded the need to control outcomes that are not mine to change.

So now I accept it and move on, not an easy task but an important one.

I'm ending this with a poem that supports Ivan Nuru's quote at the beginning of this chapter. You've probably all heard it or part of it at one time or another, but after this story, there may now be an open space within that will embrace this truth for you.

To Let Go

To let go is not to stop caring
It is to recognize I cannot do it for someone else.
To let go is not to cut myself off,
It is realizing I can't control another.
To let go is not to enable,
But to allow learning from
    natural consequences.
To let go is not to fight powerlessness,
But to accept that the outcome
    is not in my hands.
To let go is not to try to change or
Blame others,
It is to make the most of myself.
To let go is not to care for, it is to care about.
To let go is not to fix, it is to be supportive.
To let go is not to judge.
It is to allow another to be a human being.
To let go is not to try to arrange outcomes,
But to allow others to affect their own destinies.
To let go is not to be protective,
It is to permit another to face their own reality.
To let go is not to regulate anyone,
But to strive to become what I dream I can be.
To let go is not to fear less, it is to love more.

—Author Unknown

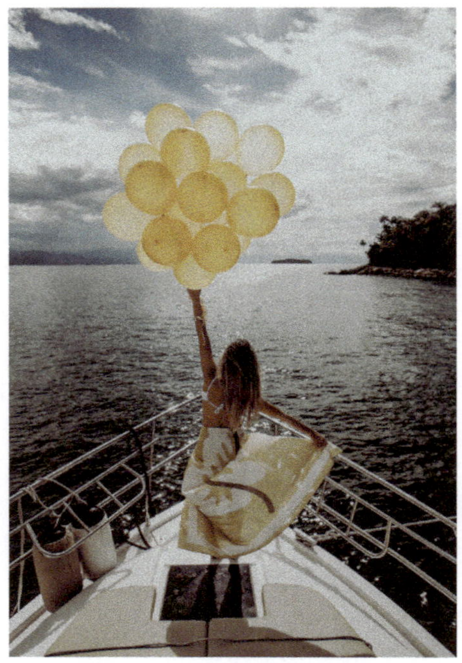

Photo by Jonathan Borba on Unsplash

Thought to ponder:

How much freedom are you going to give and honor your loved ones with to experience life on their own?

8

Chaos or Renewal

Photo by Ales Nesetril on Unsplash

With all the chaos going on in the world and opening itself wide to all our various technology screens, it seems as though everything is happening right now in our backyard. It is a lot to take in, and we wonder where the positivity and love are.

When feeling unsafe and unstable, we subconsciously try to stay alert and don't understand why we are constantly tired. It is an ongoing mental battle.

Maybe this will help.

The body's natural flow is of energy. When this even flow of energy becomes blocked because of emotions like being tense, fatigued, angry, and worried, an unbalance occurs, leaving the body feeling agitated. Taking time to be still and breathing deeply will bring a calmness to that agitation.

The color green has been known as the heart color of Mother Nature.

Whenever our world in its chaos leaves us in that agitated place, take a walk. Look closely throughout the walk, especially in the spring, where flowers are blooming and branches of trees are overflowing with leaves of all different shades of green. Mother Nature is reminding us that life on Earth is always in the process of renewal and will not be found in the chaos of the world but in the nature around us.

This calm feeling is who we really are. Love is everywhere, and it will present itself when we are still and open to receive it.

Thought to ponder:

How much of our precious energy will we give away to chaos and keep for the renewal of our true nature, which is peace?

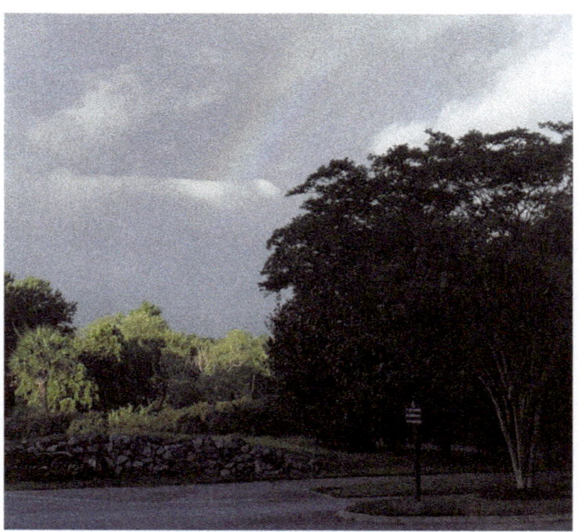

Credit / Photo by the author

9

A Call from Wisdom

Photo by Annie Spratt on Unsplash

The darkness covered me like a thick blanket, no apprehension of fear, just restraining.

Sounds of the city are echoing through my ears, making sleep seem farther to reach.

With no stillness to rest during the long active day, and no position comfortable enough to relax the energy from within, the novel I was reading before bed is now calling me back.

Finally, tiptoeing away from a bed not interested in casting a mold for slumber, I light a candle and settle in on a couch that cups my body pleasantly.

Photo by Nong V on Unsplash

Book in hand, I begin to descend into the world of Paulo Coelho's *The Alchemist*, where life brings on new adventures of the soul and the connection with All That Is!

I excitedly move from page to page, word to word, and allow my Spirit to soar, intertwining with imagination and truth.

Returning to bed, where the darkness has lifted, and the stillness embraces me with its silence, I slide in between the cool sheets.

The breeze from the fan above dances lightly over my face as my body fully stretches while releasing all inhibitions, and then…

I surrender peacefully to sleep.

Photo by DANNY G on Unsplash

Thought to ponder:

When our active days or chattered minds leave us restless, what are the ways we can love ourselves into rest?

10

Answers or Questions

The Wise Man Doesn't Give The Right Answers,
He Poses The Right Questions.

—Claude Levi-Strauss

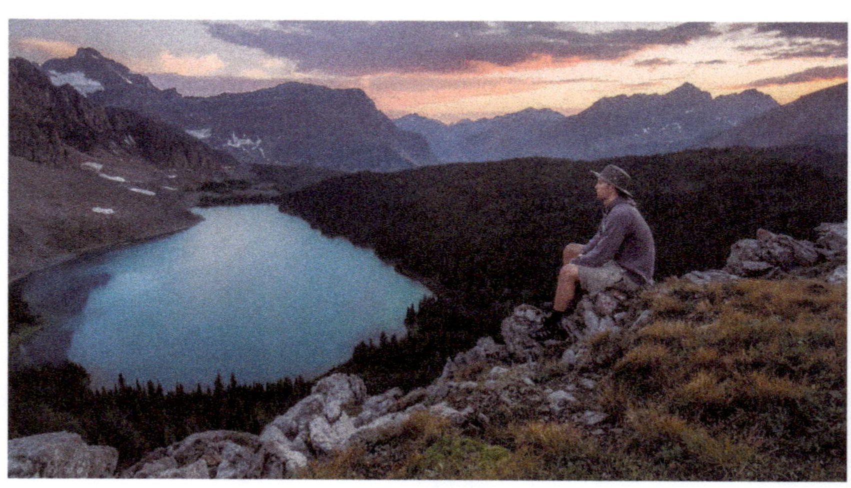

Courtesy of Pexels

There are questions we hear a lot. Like,
Why is there so much hate in the world?
I don't think I've ever heard the question,
Why is there so much Love in
the world? Have you?
Where are those kinds of positive questions?
As I pondered this, I found some.
Why is there so much beauty in the world?
Why does taking a deep breath
feel so refreshing?
Why does the first sip of something
warm on a cold morning bring
our eyes to close in comfort?
And, drinking something cold on a hot
summer day moves our lips to smile?
Why does the sound of crickets soothe
our minds to rest at night?
And the rustling of leaves brings
peace to our moments?
Why is there joy in a child's laughter?
And why does being around kittens and puppies
make the child in us want to play?
Why is it when we gaze upwards do we feel
as though our hearts have lifted?
We tend to ask why about all the negativity in
this world and the answers always begin
with: "Because we…" concluding with
a magnitude of guilt with no results.
But what if we were to switch our
question around to:
If I was to walk on this earth, just today,
As The Presence of Love, what would so
much Peace and Joy feel like?

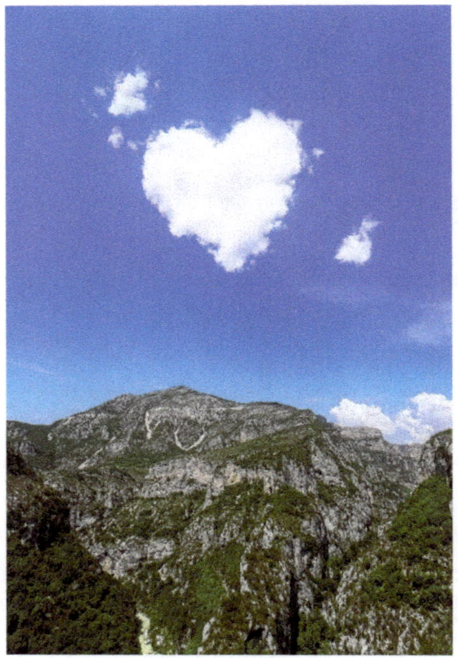

Photo by Jeremy Bezanger on Unsplash

Thought to ponder:

Reread the last two lines above, and then, close your eyes and put the answer in your heart. So whenever a negative question about ourselves and the world presents itself again, and it will, you will be ready to move out of the way and allow love to live through you.

11

How Tall Am I?

Growth: the process of evolving into who you are becoming

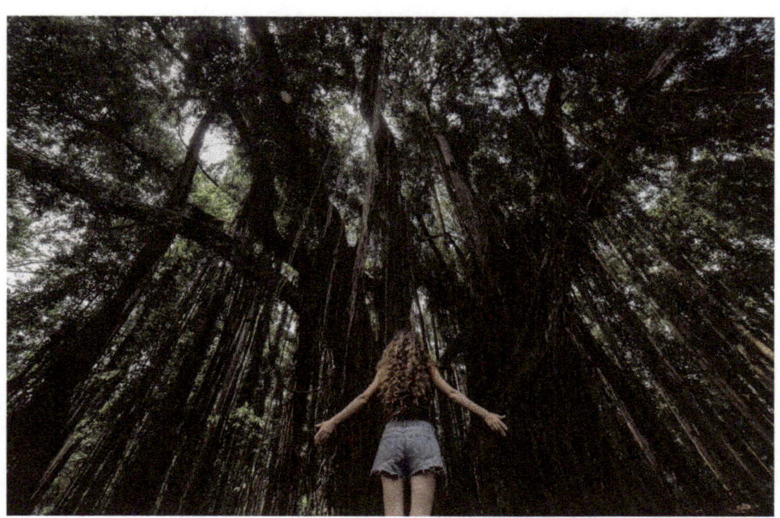

Credit Yan Krukau/ pexel.com

How tall am I as I stand feet to roots,
arms and hands reaching for the branches.
Forehead to bark, eyes closed, visualizing
my energy intertwining with a tree that
touches the sky?

I wonder if the massive tree wonders
how small it must become to
    embrace my longing.
How tall am I to bring the Earth
    into my embrace,
gathering It to my bosom, gently squeezing
the hatred, the pain, the offensiveness,
    and the sorrow from of Its pours,
To allow all the dark shadows to dissolve
    into the perfect peace of love?

TitusStaunton (https://pixabay.com)

How tall am I to stand on my tippy toes from
    the bottom of the South Pole to reach
the highest iceberg floating on the
    seas of the North Pole,
To dance in between the intense
    heat and bitter cold,
bringing awareness to these necessities
    vital to our existence?

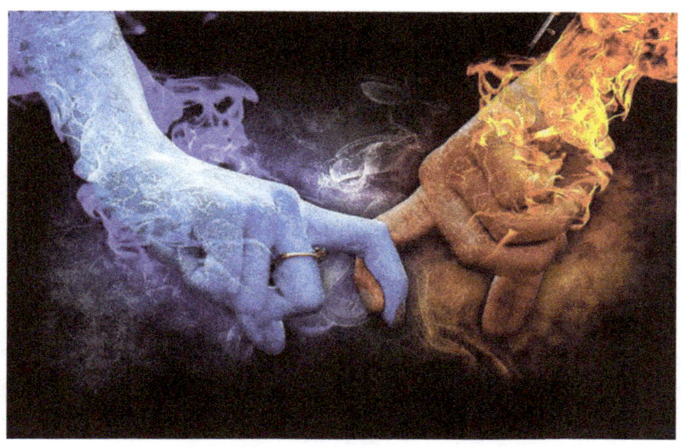

Ofjd125gk87 (https://pixabay.com)

How tall am I willing to grow to
experience the expansion
Of who I truly am?
My answer, *forever and a day.*

Elena Thomas/courtesy of Universe Connection

Thought to ponder:

How tall are you willing to grow to experience the expansion of who you truly are?

Photo by Taylor Brandon on Unsplash

12

A Forty-Five-Year-Old Poem That Has Guided Me to Authenticity

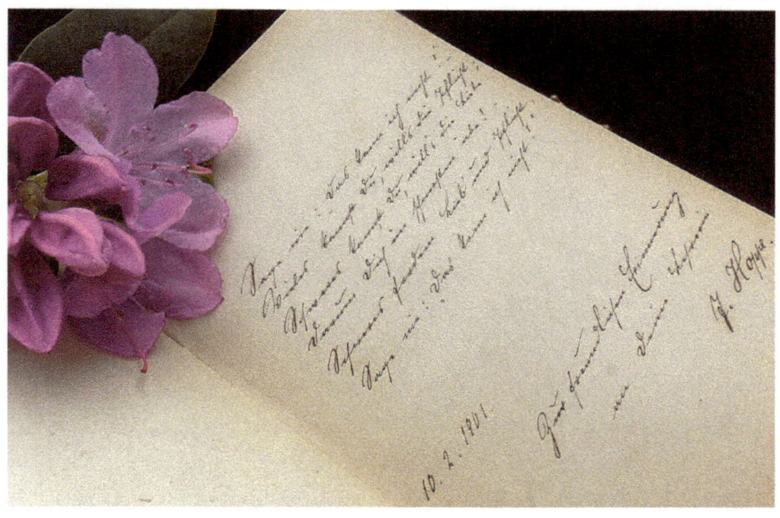

OLDIEFAN (https://pixabay.com)

When we are young and raised with a mother and a father, unconsciously, we tend to lean toward the parent we feel safest with. I was the middle child of five siblings and leaned close to my mother. She had a soft voice and a gentle touch and felt nonthreatening in all ways.

My father was the opposite. He was a difficult man to connect with and feel safe around. As I look back, I think this was because he didn't know how to show love. I would have to walk in his shoes from birth to understand why this was. But it is not for me to try and figure out why or make assumptions because only he knew.

So I move forward in gratitude, for without him, I would not be here now, living in this fascinating world and writing this story.

Jill Willington (https://pixabay.com)

My connection with my mother as a very young child was deep and personal. I thought she was the most beautiful woman in the world. We had boxes of family pictures that would come out every so often. When I was six years old and saw face pictures of Mom's youth in college and wedding pictures, I would write on the back endearing words to describe her. Then, when I made her Mother's Day cards, I'd sign my first and last name. One time, she asked me why I did that. I told her with so many kids in our family, I didn't want her to forget me.

She smiled and said, "Oh, don't worry, honey, I will never forget you," and would hold me close. It was all about the hug and how incredibly loved I felt.

My parents divorced after a very turbulent twenty-three years of marriage, and the three of us still at home were now teenagers and moved with her.

Mom had two passions. One was a nurse. She was quiet and soft-spoken and had an innate gift for easing and bringing comfort to many people in hospitals and private duty homes; they all adored her.

Mom's second passion was writing. She'd write stories about her experiences as a nurse, her younger days, and beautiful heartfelt poetry. Then she'd put them away in a box. She didn't have the confidence in herself to pursue publishing them. As I write this, I can see now that I silently followed her.

As a gift for my high school graduation, Mom gave me a poem she wrote. It was for me, about me. It was beautiful and heartfelt. I remember this was not a norm of hers, giving her writings to anyone, so I put this treasure in my special box and kept it close.

When I married and started to raise children, there were many complicated and unstable times. So I decided Mom's poem needed to come out of the box and framed. I hung it next to my bed, where her words would remind me daily that I had the strength and courage to handle whatever situation arose. As I reflected on her words, the feelings that would emerge, even after reading them thousands of times, would cover my heart with emotion, and because she knew me like no other, this poem had to represent who I was.

I became a single parent when the two younger boys were heading toward their teenage years. And there was Mom's poem still hanging beside my bed, giving me the endurance to get up in the morning and would peacefully warm my heart to rest at night.

Life got busy during those next seven years, and Mom had been ill for quite a long time. She had bouts of anxiety and preferred to stay home and live quietly. In addition, my siblings moved out of state years before, and even though Mom lived on her own, I would be there weekly to help where she needed it. During that time, we spent a lot of moments talking about our past and how we had similar experiences throughout our adult lives. It was uncanny.

When my now husband came back into my life and we started a lengthy distant relationship with him living across the country, Mom saw that we were getting serious, and she inquired, if he asked for my hand in marriage, would I? I told her that I would not leave her. She then asked if I loved him, and I said yes. She looked at me the way moms do when what they are about to say had better be heeded. "Then, you will say yes."

Five months later, he asked; I said yes, and when I told Mom, she smiled and said, "Perfect."

Mom had a relapse with her illness a couple of days before the wedding, but I was told by my siblings that I was to concentrate on the wedding and that they would take care of her. My brother later mentioned that in rehab, Mom talked about her excitement with the navy captain I was to marry and would not miss it for anything.

And she proved that. Even though my sister had to hold her up while I walked down the aisle, she was there. I looked into her eyes, saying, "Mom, please sit down!"

And her eyes spoke back with a confirmed, "Not on your life!"

As we prepared to move a week later to the East Coast with my youngest, now a senior in high school, in tow, saying goodbye to Mom was more than difficult. She and I have always had a silent connection far beyond words, and I innately knew that this would be the last time we'd physically be together, and so did she. So I told her to say the word, and she would come with us.

Mom answered no and then added, "Terry, I have one piece of advice to take with you. Remember the choices I made in life, and do the opposite."

At that moment, I was confused. She saw this but just touched my hand. We hugged, and I said, "I love you," and placed her in my siblings' care.

I reflected on Mom's advice on the two-day car drive to our new home. Intertwining our life experiences and their similarities made me catch my breath more than once.

I realized that little girl who leaned close to her mother and felt safe chose to follow in her footsteps. That's what love does; you carry the good, the bad, and the ugly, right?

Mom taught me differently. I am to carry the good and learn from the unhealthy and that there is no ugly—just growth and expansion.

Mom passed away within two weeks after my second husband and I married.

As my siblings and I finished cleaning out her apartment and the door was to be closed for the last time, I remembered that I hadn't checked if her plants needed watering. We left them behind for the next occupant, so I ran back in. Mom used to put little treasures she had found on the soil of her plants, and as I went to the last one, there was a treasure just for me. It was a small white porcelain wishing well with hand-painted flowers around the well, and on the little roof, the words *Forget Me Not* were written. As I picked it up and brushed off the dirt, a memory floated through my mind's eye. It was the time as a little girl I had said to her that I had hoped she would not forget me, and her last physical message to me was, "Forget me not." I felt it was her way of saying always close, never forgotten.

In the past twenty-two years since her transition, every choice that may come to me as negative or fearful, I first ponder what Mom's choice would be, and then I would choose the opposite. Because of this, my life has been nothing but remarkable and full of growth.

I have a voice memo app that I recorded Mom's poem in my voice. I have used this poem at times after meditations to soothe moments of uncertainty about why I am here. And now, when emotions stir, I am grateful for her wise words and the deep desire she carried for me to experience life to the fullest and to share the truth of who I am with others.

Photographer Galia Gty/Israel

Terry—A Graduation Wish For You (June 13, 1974)

To want for you, only the best
That life can give
Is a natural wish for a Beautiful
Daughter on Graduation.
But may I add; know that your future
Will hold bits and pieces of adversities
Sometimes, even broken dreams
And tattered hearts
Compensate for this by
Sprinkling each day with little bits of love
The future will then have accumulated
These scraps into a Mountainous Treasure
And no one may claim it
For it is a part of you
Share it, Honey
With those who have never loved
For it will then grow even taller
And its peak will penetrate the Heavens
From this Graduation on
Commence your Savings with Love
You will then have accomplished
That Goal for which you were created.

—Mom

My mother's high school graduation picture

Thank you, Mom. You were and are an inspiration. Your wisdom lives through me.

Thought to ponder:
Who is it in the journey of your life thus far who has given you inspiration or wisdom? What a priceless gift it would be to share this with them while they are still with us.

13

The $10,000 Call

Courtesy of The Gold Gator/Etsy

When the boys were young, we had our school morning routines. This day was no different. We were almost out the door when one of the kids yelled from their bedroom.

"Hey, Mom, do we have any more cardboard? I have a hole in the bottom of my shoe?"

I yelled back. "In the garage. Bring me the shoe, and I'll get a piece to fit it."

As we all scampered into the car, the three older boys settled in and were taking inventory, ensuring they had everything, and the youngest buckled in his car seat; one of them said, "What's for dinner tonight, Mom?"

Knowing the response, I said, "Chicken."

All three chimed in like an out-of-tune choir. "Again?"

Even the youngest piped in. "Again, Mama?"

"Kids, it's the best I can do on our budget. But, hey, I know, I'll make chicken spaghetti. That sounds yummy right?"

Sounds of crickets.

"Kids?"

"Um…okay," one uttered.

"And I'll make oatmeal cookies for dessert! How about that?"

Crickets chirping again.

"Oh, come on, boys, work with me here." I pleaded.

We pulled up to the school, and out the door, they flew. I looked at the sweet little face in the backseat. My son's eyes had a sad expression as he said, "I don't like oatmeal cookies, Mama."

"I know you don't, sweety. So let's stop at the store, and I'll pick up some chocolate chips, and we'll make some yummy cookies today."

"Yay! Okay!" he said as he gently kicked his feet forward and back on the car seat. Little ones are so easy to please.

Courtesy of Congerdesign/https://pixabay.com

Our local radio station, KLZZ, played on the way to school and back. They had a contest going on. You had to listen to two songs back to back and wait until *after* the second song ended to call in, and if you were the tenth caller, $10,000 would be yours! So after a week of this contest, today would be the day they would play both songs back to back before noon.

People were calling in, saying their families were taking shifts during the days and nights so they wouldn't miss "the moment" in anticipation of winning.

They would say the radio station was teasing them by playing one of the songs and then not the other, etc. I found it all fascinating, so I kept listening.

We ran some errands after dropping the kids off and got home around 10:30 a.m. I wanted to keep listening but knew *Sesame Street* would be on soon, which was my son's favorite show. *Oh well.*

After putting groceries away and throwing some laundry in, I looked for my son and found him quietly playing with his toys in his room. *Huh?* By this time, it was almost 11:30 a.m. *Okay, I'll sneak away and turn on KLZZ to listen to the final half hour.*

I decided to make cookies and stay close to the radio (it was in the mideighties, and there were no cellphones or stereos in the kitchen, just a simple radio on the counter). People were calling between songs, saying things like, "Hurry up, I called work and told them I couldn't be in before noon" and "I have to take my dog for a walk...please hurry!" I was shaking my head.

Hearing the ringing in my ear

Five minutes to noon, the first song came on. I thought, *This is it! It's going to happen!* Then the second one played. Oh my gosh! The phone was on the wall, an arm's reach away. I glanced at it and thought, *Maybe I should try.*

I saw the picture float by my mind of putting the piece of cardboard in my son's shoe this morning and then the conversation with the kids in the car, not at all happy about having chicken spaghetti for dinner. Yes, money was very tight; our bill collectors could tell you all about it.

The second song ended. I reached for the phone and dialed. (Yes, you actually had to dial a rotary phone. It took forever!)

Busy. Again, I dialed... busy.

One more time... ringing? It's ringing?

I must have the wrong number. As I was ready to hang up and try again, I heard a voice in my head say, *Don't hang up. Just stay on.*

Then the prayers started. "Listen, Spirit, you know how hard we work here. It's not like we're sitting around watching TV all day, right?"

The phone is still ringing, and I'm pacing back and forth (the phone cord could only go so far), still talking to Spirit, "I usually don't ask for things, although if you could help us out here, I'll give $1,000 of it away to someone who needs it, like us. Winning this money would help so much! We could buy the kids new shoes and have something more than chicken and macaroni and cheese for dinner. And we could pay our bills!"

The phone picked up.

Photo by Fringer Cat on Unsplash

THE DJ.	KLZZ. (Gulp!)
ME.	You're going to tell me I'm the ninth caller, right?

THE DJ. Nope…you are the tenth caller…and…just won…$10,000!

ME. Oh my gosh! You're kidding? I actually won $10,000?

I was pacing frantically and breathing heavily!

THE DJ. Yes! You won! Congratulations! Who am I speaking to?

I could barely get my name out and felt light-headed from all the heavy breathing. (At this moment, my three-year-old came out, looking startled, and tears started forming in his eyes.)

ME, yelling. Terry!

THE DJ. You okay?

ME. Yes! Yes! I'm okay!

THE DJ. Well, Terry, what are you going to do with the $10,000?

(Every time his voice raised when he mentioned the money, my heart pounded and fluttered.)

ME. I don't know. Um…we have family in New York I have never met. We could go there. I could take the whole family out for dinner, and we could get dessert! (I heard myself inside say, "Why did you say that? This is $10,000 we're talking about here." I did a mental hit on my forehead.)

THE DJ. Well, okay! (Trying to sound excited for me) Congratulations again, Terry, and stay on the line so we can get your information.

Me.	Okay! And thank you so much! This is incredible! Thank you!

The DJ had put me on hold before the last thank you, but I was a mess, and my poor little boy was hugging my leg like it was going to fall off and kept saying, "Mommy, are you okay?"

I stroked his head gently and smiled; our eyes met, and he smiled back.

The sweet woman who took my information was wonderful at calming me down and told me I had to wait a month for the check and gave me a date to stop by the radio station to pick it up.

After we said goodbye and I thanked her for the one hundredth time, I plopped down on the chair, brought my breathing back to normal, and stared out to space. What just happened here? My son climbed up on my lap and nestled in, patting my back with his little hand like small ones do to comfort us.

On the table was a piece of paper with the information the woman had given me. I picked up the pencil and wrote what $10,000 looked like. I'm a visual person, and seeing it made it real. Who sees $10,000 at one time? Not us. I started tearing up in gratitude when I finished and looked at it. Crying never felt so good.

The day we all went out to play

The six of us were up early and out the door with a check for $10,000 in hand. The bank was our first stop and then breakfast, and what a breakfast we had. We told the boys we'd be heading to Toys R Us after we ate.

They stopped eating and looked at each other wide-eyed. We added that they would each be given $20 to shop. Again, back in the eighties, that was a lot of money for ten-, seven-, and three-year-olds. They were shocked and quickly finished up and said, "Done! We're ready," one of my happiest moments that day.

The rest of the day was like a dream—new clothes and shoes for everyone. We filled our cart with all kinds of yummy food at the grocery store and got off our bill collector's *way*-past-due payment list.

We were ecstatic to see money left over to keep us afloat for a while.

Now, who was I going to give $1000 to?

My mom lived close by, and so did my younger sister. She and her husband had three girls at the time. We would help each other with food and childcare when needed. All of us closely counted our pennies. So I decided to go to the bank and get $1000 in twenty-dollar bills. I put $500 each in two envelopes. Mom and my sister didn't know about this, and I was excited.

The first stop was the clinic where my mom worked. She was surprised to see me but was busy. So I hugged her and said I just wanted to drop something off at her desk. There was a bit of a surprise on her face, but she hugged me back and said she'd call later. It was tough to keep a straight face, but the call was going to be exciting, so I put a little heart on the envelope and wrote, "Thank you for being my mom. I love you."

Then, I went to my sister's. She was starting dinner, and her husband and the kids were hanging around the kitchen. I thought, *This is going to be fun!*

When I came in, she was surprised, and I told her I just wanted to give her something. As I handed the envelope to her, she whispered, "What's this?"

Courtesy of Karolina Grabowska (https://pexels.com)

I whispered back, “It’s just a little something I wanted to give you guys for helping us the way you do…open it!”

When she did and saw all those $20, tears started forming.

She looked at her husband, he moved forward, and the kids followed and went ahead of him to look in the envelope. Mouths widened. My sister took the money out and laid each twenty, one by one, on the kitchen table, and the kids started counting, giggling, and jumping up and down.

My sister waved her hand in front of her eyes so she wouldn’t cry, but it didn’t work.

In this case, what I learned was money is a tool. It is to be respected, enjoyed, and shared, and its value is in the hands of the beholder.

No one has ever seen a U-Haul pulled by a hearse; it’s not going with us when we leave this world, so why not use it as the gift it is?

Winning $10,000 was a fun experience, but sharing it and seeing what happened to others when I did solidifies that what feeds me is when I give in joy, I experience joy. This way of living is a part of who I am now and never ceases to continue to provide me with heart flutters each time I put giving into action.

Thought to ponder:

What experiences have you had that because of you someone feels gifted?

14

"Don't Blink"

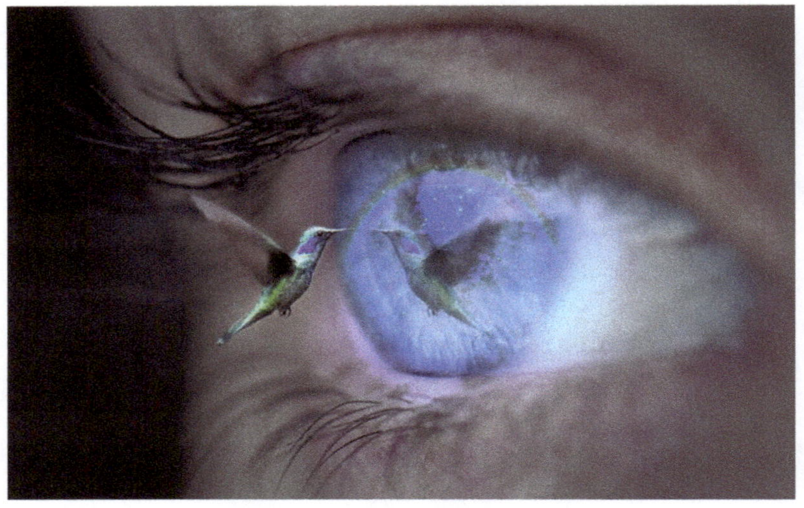

Courtesy of https://pixabay.com

Life goes by in a blink of an eye. Appreciate the moments.

—ABINASH

Music is like therapy for me. It energizes, calms, brings me to a place of pondering, and teaches me about life. Depending on my mood, I play the music that feeds me at the time. The other morning, after a long walk in the woods, I decided to listen to artists with more of a reflective genre while making breakfast. Then, Kenny Chesney's "Don't Blink" came on. Memories of my life started playing back as I listened to each line.

Don't Blink
By Kenny Chesney

I turned on the evening news
Saw an old man being interviewed
Turning a hundred and two today
Asked him what's the secret to life
He looked up from his old pipe
Laughed and said all I can say is
Don't blink, just like that, you're six years old
And you take a nap. And you wake up,
and you're twenty-five
Then your high school sweetheart
becomes your wife
Don't blink, you just might miss your babies
Growing like mine did
Turning into moms and dads next thing
you know, your better half of fifty years is
there in bed
And you're praying God takes you instead
Trust me, friend, a hundred years
go faster than you think
So, don't blink
I was glued to my TV when it looked
like he looked at me
And said best start putting first things first
'Cause when your hourglass runs out of sand
You can't flip it over and start again
Take every breath God gives you
for what it's worth.
So, don't blink
So I've been trying to slow it down

I've been trying to take it in
In this here today gone tomorrow
world we're living in
So don't blink.

Written by Casey Beathard, Chris Wallin
Sung by Kenny Chesney

I attended a Catholic school for the first two years, where uniforms were expected. I went to public school in my third year, and my mom took us all out to get new clothes. In the early morning of my first day, I was so excited to wear my new dress and patent leather shoes that I quietly got up when it was still dark and got ready for school. I sat on the couch with my new dress neatly on, a new lunch box sitting by my side, and waited. When my mom walked out of her room, she was surprised to see me.

"Terry, what are you doing up?"

I responded, "Waiting to go to school."

She smiled and said, "It's only 5:30 a.m. School doesn't start for four hours. You should go back to bed to rest for the big day!"

Don't blink.

When the kids were babies, they were "Aww, so adorable." Even though as they got to be school age, there were many times of wiping the sweat off my brow and staying up until after midnight making cupcakes, after a child remembered he forgot to tell me he had volunteered me to do this for the next day, as we said good night.

Don't blink.

Then when they became teenagers, they were not so adorable.

Picture this: Walking into the kitchen one morning, my middle son, high school age with attitude, was making eggs over the stove. In a cheery voice, I said, "Good morning, hon!"

Not looking up, he said, "Mom! Why do you have to make conversation with me first thing in the morning!" (Grrrrrr.)

"Hon, all I said was good morning."

Still not looking up, "That's a start of a conversation, not interested."

Frustrated, I noticed that he had jeans on, if one could say they were on, with the waist of the pants hanging almost under his tush. (Not meanly, if anybody reading still does this, no judging here, but why?)

I then calmly said, "Well, pull your pants up!"

Still, without looking up (I mean, how long does it take to make a couple of eggs?), he gently jumped up and down once, and they fell to the ground. Me...*grrrrrrrrrrr*. Mental slap behind his head as I walked past.

Don't blink.

After graduating from high school, he moved away to a college in Sacramento. I saw him only during holidays in those years. Toward the end of his final year, we met at a mutual friend's house for dinner. I was distant from the door but could see him being welcomed in.

I saw this handsome young man, hair combed, shirt pressed and tucked in, in slacks(?) that fit perfectly and with a belt! *What the! This is my son?* Tears started to bubble up on their own. He's a young man? When did *this* happen? He gave me an amazing tight hug when we saw each other, which brought me back to the room in joy. During dinner, he was honestly polite and spoke knowledgeably and respectfully. I had to keep blinking and pinching myself to realize that he had grown up.

That aggravating teenager, now a hardworking neurologist as chief of staff for two hospitals, has a teenager and another right behind her. He is one of the kindest and most caring people you would ever want to meet.

Don't blink.

The surprising changes from boys to men happened with all of my boys at different times, but blinking is something I did pretty often, especially when they weren't home for months.

My two oldest sons were always mischievous. I remember working at a carnival booth with the teens to raise money. The twins were done and went to get on some rides. About an hour later, I saw one of them running past the booth as if he was being chased and yelled, "Hi, Mom!"

And then, the other ran past, waving to me with a few friends not far behind him. Not even a second later, three policemen were running just as fast to catch them. Apparently, a misunderstanding between some teens from another school escalated, and it wasn't pretty. I took a breath, rolled my eyes, and said to the woman next to me, "Here we go again."

Years later, when the second oldest received an honorable discharge from the Air Force and married, he held his first child right after birth. His tears spoke volumes of how he had matured and would love and protect this child with all his heart.

Don't blink.

When my youngest joined the Peace Corps after college and went to Madagascar for two years, it was life-changing for him. The experience of living in a small village with no electricity or running water changed this boy from feeling entitled and with an attitude to someone with a deep appreciation for life. He could not wait to step out and change the world with compassion, humility, and a zest for experiences.

And he did. In the beginning, he helped small businesses to achieve success and is now training to become a nurse to give his gifts of compassion to those in need. I was in awe of who he had become.

Don't blink.

The takeaway: You see, I believe there is a movie projector that lives in our hearts. It collects the stories from our lives and waits patiently for the opportunity to be clicked back on to help us feel the abundance of those experiences again.

It is mind-blowing to see my second oldest closing in on fifty in a few years and the other boys not too far behind, especially when I look into their eyes and the movie projector starts to play again in fast motion from the days of their youth.

We have rare and beautiful treasures flowing through our lives all the time that will become memories before we can even blink. So if we can slow down, take it all in, and take every breath we are given for what it's worth, as Kenny expresses through his song, we can capture these moments in full awareness of the gifts we have been given.

Thought to ponder:

What treasures have been flowing through your lives and being captured in your movie projector?

Don't blink.

15

"A Calmness That Knows No Fear"

-BENIGHTED

Photo by InWay/courtesy of https://pixabay.com

The human mind can only imagine,
Calmness without fear.
But Spirit knows only this way of being.

Living within us,
Sharing the same space is
The human mind and Spirit.
How can this be?

An erratic emotional mess
Being tossed around like a massive
tree in a hurricane.
While the calmness that knows no fear,
Rests in the eye like a feather on still water.

How can fear and calmness share the same space
And not embrace each other?
Which one is more powerful?
And...Who decides?

Photo by Yoann Boyer on Unsplash

Thought to ponder:
How could you bring calmness to your fears?

16

Ten Pictures, Ten Words, and Ten Stories

The pictures we choose to surround ourselves with calls to connect with the place of remembering. I hope you enjoy this piece as much as I had in creating it.

1) A graceful, intimate moment of communing with all of creation.

Yaroslav Shuraev / Pixel.com

2) Living a powerfully creative essential life, from the inside out

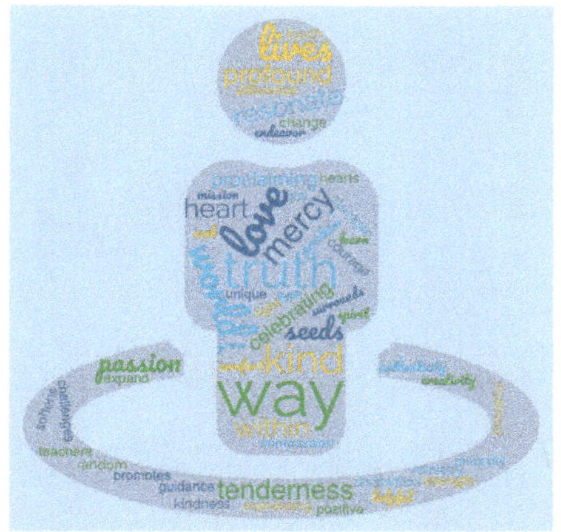

These words float around inside, reminding me of my truth (created by the author)

3) Preparing for their wedding, where the two shall become one

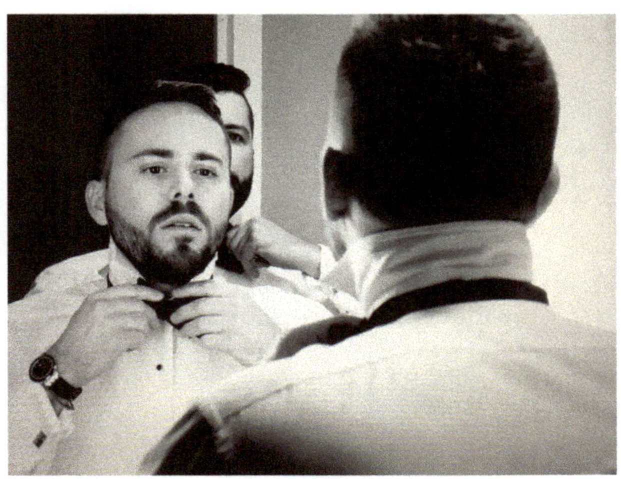

My youngest son (behind) and his beautiful spouse on their wedding day (photo by author)

4) Sometimes, reading between the words is the message we seek.

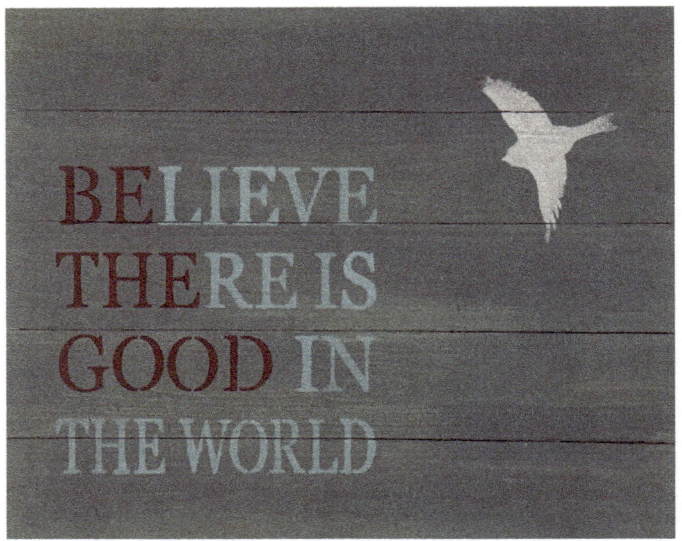

Photo hanging in our home (by the author)

5) Struggles seem real until the wind blows the veil away.

Photo by Bernie Blekfeld - White Winds/photo hanging in our home

6) Walking down the same path from 2000 years ago, priceless

An incredible, memorable trip I took alone in Jerusalem, Israel (taken by the author)

7) Uplifting words to reflect on for healing in the hospital

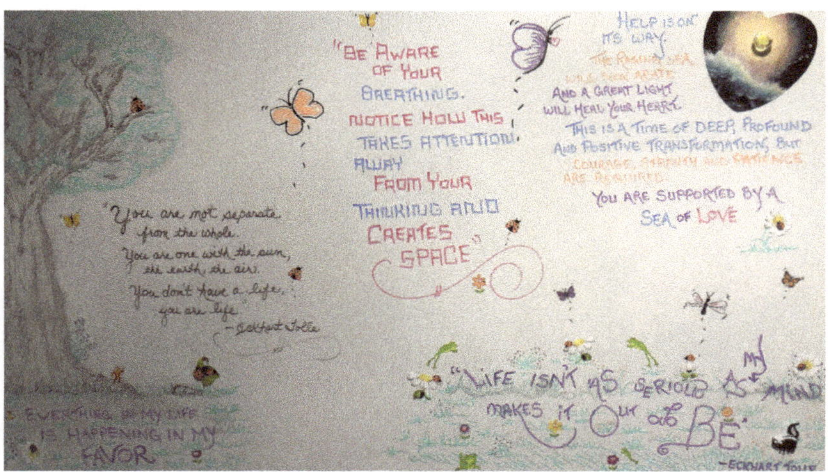

After a difficult nine-hour surgery, I put this up in my husband's room (art by the author)

8) The connection with nature is undeniably real, exquisite, and beautiful.

When this puzzle was finished, I was in awe
(Bev Doolittle: Western Camoflauge Artist)

9) The warmth of her father's hand felt safe and peaceful.

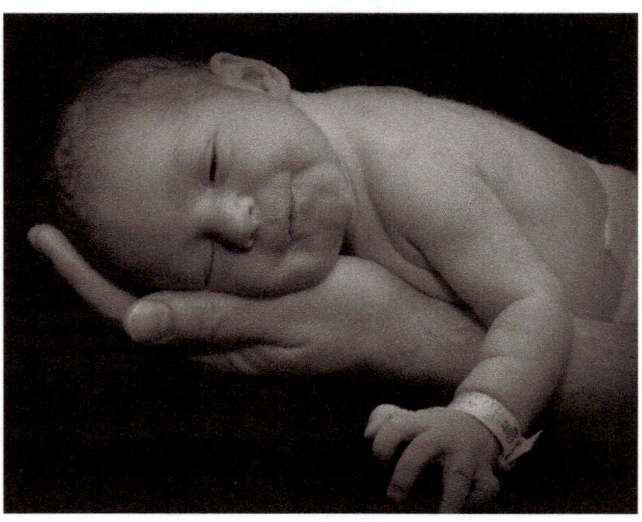

My oldest son's firstborn child the day she was born

10) In gratitude for the support from my beautiful readers.

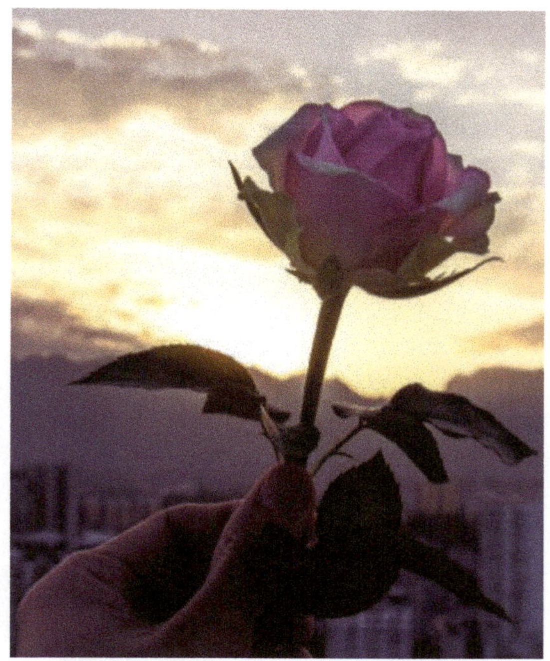

Thank you is not enough. Photographer Galia Gty/Israel

Thought to ponder:

What stories do the pictures you surround yourself with tell of your remembrance?

17

Sorrow's Transformation into Joy

Mbll (https://pixabay.com)

Joy and sorrow are the light and shade of life;
without light and shade no picture is clear.

—Hazrat Inayat Khan

Thanksgiving morning in 1959

It was early Thanksgiving morning in 1959. The four of us kids had gathered in one bedroom to play board games while waiting for the Thanksgiving parade to come on TV. We could already smell the turkey cooking. Mom was eight-and-a-half months pregnant and didn't get a lot of sleep and had put it in a few hours before. Our nine-month-old sister was sleeping in her crib in our parent's room across the hall, so we had to be quiet.

My eight-year-old brother was relaxing on his bed, reading a comic book. My two older sisters, Kathy, six and a half, and the other, five, and myself, three, decided on another game, the phone game. It was calm and fun at the same time.

There were electrical outlets on each side of the connecting rooms. We found if one of us was in one room and had their ear up to the outlet, they could hear perfectly when the person in the next room had their mouth close to the outlet and spoke, thus calling it the phone game.

Kathy stayed in the room with my older brother and chose to speak first. My sister and I went into the other bedroom and shut the door. Putting our ears as close to the socket hole as possible, Kathy whispered something. We could hardly hear her and asked her to speak louder. She did, but we still couldn't make out what she was saying.

One more time, my sister asked her to speak louder. At some point, Kathy had put something in her mouth, and when she took a deep breath, the object lodged in her throat. We could hear her choking and gasping for air. We stood still and looked at each other.

We could hear the other bedroom door slam against the wall and my brother screaming to my parents that Kathy was choking. My sister and I still didn't move. There was a lot of commotion. We could hear our dad yell to my brother to run as fast as he could to our neighbor, a nurse, and bring her back quickly. We heard Mom soothing Kathy in some way as she gasped.

My sister and I came out of the room when we heard people coming into the house, and I went where everyone was in the kitchen. I stood back against the kitchen's lower cabinets, watching as Kathy was being held upside down by her feet by my dad as he shook her body, and our neighbor slapped her back to try to unlodge the object. At the time, I didn't know she was unconscious; she just looked like she was sleeping. No one shooed me out, nor did I feel any sense of fear. I'm sure there was plenty, but I think it's because Kathy's face looked calm and peaceful that I, too, felt peace.

However, the object did not come out. Someone had called an ambulance because within minutes, the medics rushed in and took Kathy to the hospital. It was then my siblings and I were ushered into another room.

Kathy died on the way to the hospital, on Thanksgiving in 1959.

Toward the end of Kathy's funeral, a few days later, Mom began to have labor pains and was taken to the hospital. She told me once that as she walked up and down the hall to relieve the pain from the contractions, a doctor had noticed her as he walked by. He joyfully said to her, "Don't look so sad. You look like you just came back from a funeral. You're having a baby!" She smiled at him, and he moved on.

My little brother was born a week after Kathy passed, and I remember being so excited. Mom walked into the house with him and sat on the couch so we could all take a peek. I thought he was so small and so cute! Because of all that went on the week before, there wasn't time to get a crib, so Mom made a bed from a shoe box and placed him in an open dresser drawer. The drawer she put him in was a little lower than my height, so I could look at him all I wanted and did. I remember my older brother running in the room and asking Mom what his name was because the neighborhood kids were outside and wanted to know.

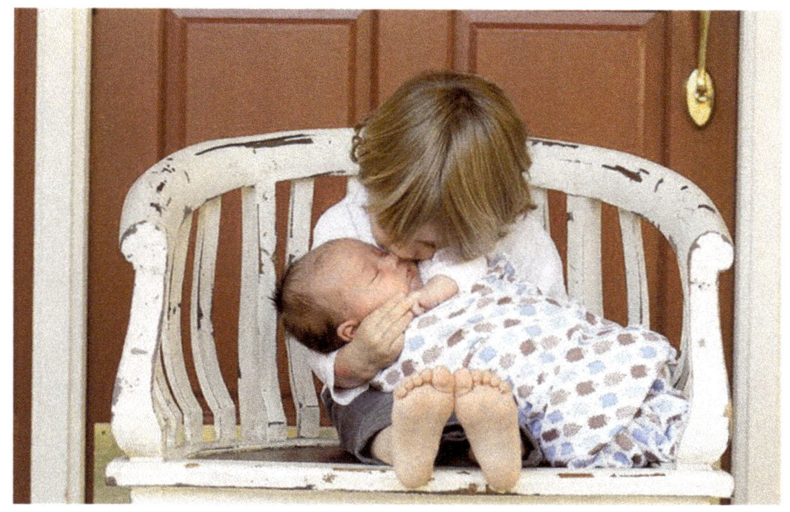

999/https://pixabay.com

Randy's presence in our family

My new baby brother was named Edgar Roland, after our dad, but Mom didn't want him to go by that name. So she said, "Tell them your little brother's name is Randy."

So my brother ran outside yelling. "Our little brother's name is Randy!" I could hear clapping and loud, happy whistles, and when I looked at Mom, she was smiling lovingly at her new baby. I felt joy inside.

As I write this, I am amazed at how aware I was and the clarity of this experience at just three years old. It appears this all happened yesterday.

Our house was full of neighbors, friends, and relatives throughout the week. Everyone wanted to see and hold this little miracle. I say miracle because after my younger sister was born, Mom's doctor cautioned her that after having five babies in seven years, her small body had had enough. So when she became pregnant with Randy, he was concerned for her health. But to his surprise, she carried him well and with the birth and healing afterward, henceforth, a miracle in the making.

Randy was a godsend. He brought so much joy to our family from birth. Mom said he was a happy baby, and we all could not love him enough. He was adorable, sweet, and very loving.

I remember Mom telling me that Ran had to have eye surgery at four years old. His eyes would have to be completely covered for a few days, and he had to stay in the hospital. When she walked into the room to visit Randy and saw the other children crying, she heard him soothing them, saying, "Don't cry, it will be okay. Your mommy and daddy will be here soon."

Even today, these traits of compassion and empathy and the desire to help others exist. We have always called him the heart of the family, and indeed, he was and still is.

As Randy got older, the sense of humor he carried would change a room full of sadness into lightness and joy. We'd be sad one moment and the next, crying with laughter. He could work a room like nobody's business, and no one wanted to leave. That's how contagious my little brother was and is. It's as if this was his purpose for coming into this world, and he nailed it.

To this day, whenever Randy's name is mentioned, a huge grin rests on people's faces, and they talk about his kindness, compassion, and crazy, beautiful sense of humor. Being around him brought a lightness that people craved, even today.

While writing this story, I stopped and tried to put myself in Mom's place many times. I didn't realize the immense heart pain she must have endured burying one child and the incredible joy of a new birth days later. It's as if those two stand-alone emotions intertwined and held her up in strength and courage. How could this be humanly possible? Mom was a small, quiet woman, but to me, her strength is one you only hear in stories of unbelievable bravery.

Kathy's picture was always on Mom's dresser, but she never spoke about her. But it wasn't an off-limits subject; someone would occasionally bring Kathy up when we were older, which was okay; Mom showed and shared warmth in those moments.

On Thanksgiving each year, we would always go to the cemetery to bring flowers and the happy pictures us kids would make and give our respects. The rest of the day we'd spend with family and friends, celebrating and giving thanks. I always appreciated this because I learned that even in the most devastating moments, when taking time to rest in the light of gratitude, it will surround us and lift our hearts in peace.

It wasn't until I was an adult that Mom and I talk about Kathy, but never in-depth. Although over the years, when the box of pictures of us as small kids came out, we thought it was uncanny how Kathy's face and Randy's looked almost identical. The positivity of this thought brought a soft smile to Mom's lips. To imagine Kathy's Spirit would have moved into my mother's womb when she passed and, hence, Randy was born gave us peace.

Now, isn't *that* something to ponder?

Photo by Andra C. Taylor Jr. on Unsplash

Final thoughts:

Because of the amount of time I spent writing and rewriting this story, I thought maybe it wasn't my story to tell. So I sat down with a few wise sages and explained my dilemma. They told me it was indeed my story to share because I was there in the experience. But I was to tell it from my perspective, not my mother's. An *ah-ha moment* then appeared.

Writing from a child's perspective was not so difficult. Writing as if I was my mom pretty much left me emotionally unstable for a few weeks. But I was reassured that Mom and Kathy were now together, and the love they share far surpasses human understanding. Upon hearing this, I breathed a long sigh of relief and gratitude.

And last, but not least, is Randy. I feel our lives would have had an enormous emptiness and a sense of sadness would have hovered over our hearts for years, especially for my mom, without the joy of Randy's presence in our lives. He is the essential piece of the puzzle that completes and shines light on our family dynamics. And the gratitude continues.

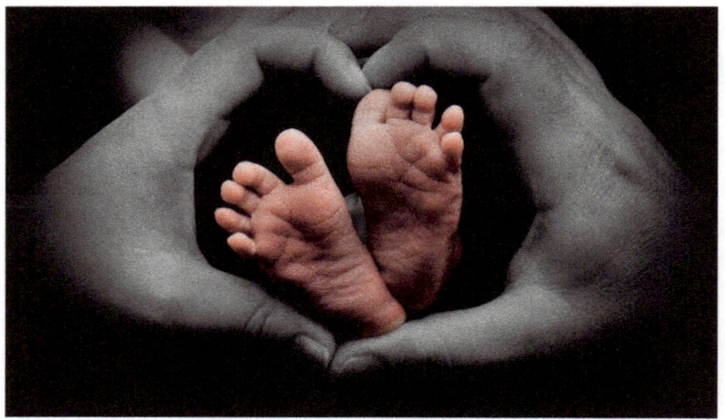

Courtesy of John P. Salvatore

18

"Write Your Sad Times in Sand. Write Your Good Times in Stone. (George Bernard Shaw)"

Frank Winkler/https://pixabay.com

It's usually the other way around. Isn't it?

For me, it is.

I wonder why that is.

The good times bring joy, and when we ponder those times, the feeling moves through us again as if we are still experiencing the moment, and the cells are refreshed. True?

I think that's why many of us, including children, reread books, rewatch movies, and bring up those stories around the dinner table, to feel the energy of happiness again.

One day on a walk, my friend, Patrice, was walking her dog a little distance ahead. Her border collie's name was Bailey and has been trained not to leave the yard without her owner. When we've seen each other, she would stand up and wag her tail but, with frustration, would not move. I could also tell she was young by the way she'd look up at her owner, walking with a lightness and excitement about her surroundings.

Bailey turned around and saw me and then stopped and pulled the leash my way. Patrice turned, saw me, waved, and pulled Bailey to go her way. The pup would not have it; she stopped and pulled her owner my way, not wanting to lose sight of me.

I was smiling, instantly feeling joy at the excitement of watching how the sweet animal wanted to come to me. Patrice finally stopped. I usually ask if it's okay to pet a dog when I see one, but we know each other, so when I got down on my knees, Bailey gently but excitingly nuzzled into my neck. I was in heaven.

Patrice apologized because the morning dew was still on the dog's paws, and she saw my clothes getting dirty. I told her that's what washing machines were for. We both laughed and agreed. As I kept petting and saying loving words to Bailey, we were in sort of communion together, and the energy felt between us was as one, and I didn't want to leave.

As I got up, Bailey was satisfied, and I thanked the owner for allowing me to have a moment with her pride and joy. I walked away feeling so serene and content that this connection seemed to have filled a void I didn't even know existed. I could sense this energy as being different, and how it contented me was profound. Even as I write now and remember the experience, I feel a wave of peace.

The only thing I can think of was that I felt alone and out of sorts during my walk, even though I was grateful for the day.

This story may sound insignificant, but it is the *feeling* and the *energy* that moved me and rested in my heart and in my cells and solidified, becoming a part of my energy too.

It *was* a *good time* that should be *written in stone* for me. So I wondered why I would choose to write my sorrows in stone and my joys in the sand. I think it's time to change!

We can learn from the sad, complex stories we write and read. Those too are an essential part of our growth, but then after those are written, let's turn to the stories we have written in stone, the joy we have experienced, and rest in them afterward, returning us to our precise alignment, love.

DigiPD/https://pixabay.com

Thought to ponder:
Do you write your good times in stone or in the sand?

19

"Be Kind whenever Possible. It Is Always Possible. (Dalai Lama)"

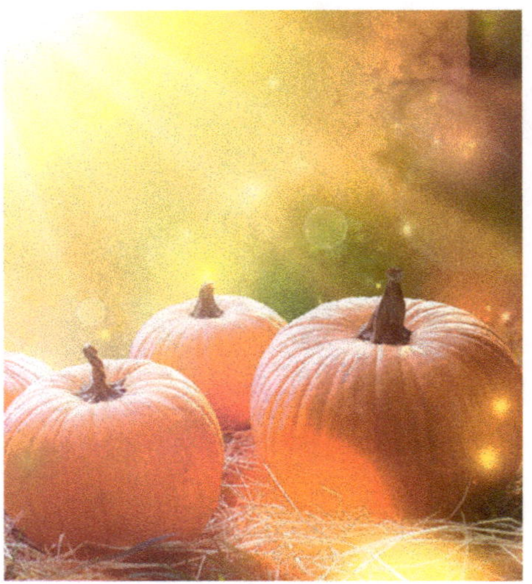

EdgarCayce.org

A Thanksgiving Thought to Ponder
May we allow the Pure Light that
created us live and
breathe through our thoughts,
actions, stomachs, and
hearts today. Reminding us of
the gift that we are.

That it is definitely okay to have extra helpings
of mashed potatoes, stuffing, lots
    of gravy, and pumpkin
pie smothered in whipped cream.

Remember, you're taking in food
    for the One who created
all that is, so you may want to adjust
    your belt for that or
skip the belt and wear elastic today.

What better day to give Thanks to
    you than on a day when
everyone's hearts are wide open to
    take in this incredible
feeling of giving, receiving, and love.

Sending joy and delicious conversations

Thought to ponder:
What fills your heart with gratitude?

20

Santa's Spirit Grows

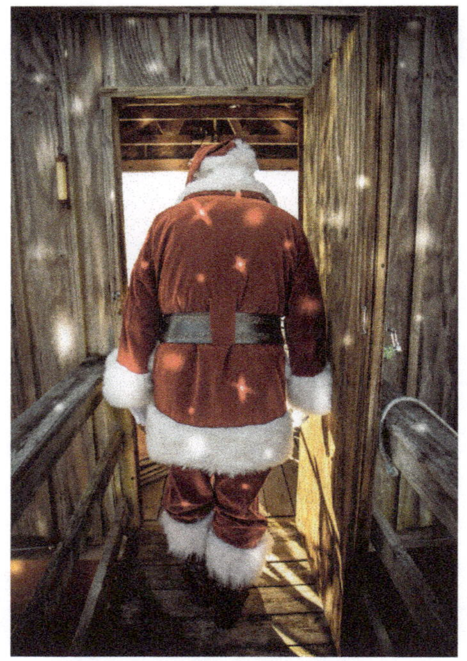

How I love this picture. It reflects my heart!
(Photo by LuAnn Hunt on Unsplash)

A few years ago, a friend of mine wrote me a letter about her fears and worries that this may be her daughter's last year believing in Santa Claus. Rylie was turning nine the following year and was always excited about Christmas and felt a closeness and love for Santa. Since my boys were all grown, she asked me if I had any pointers to share that may help both of them.

Here was my response: "You know, Cheryl, when the time comes that Rylie comes up to you and tells you she knows the truth about Santa, it could be an excellent opportunity to teach her what the gift of Christmas is all about. You could start by saying, 'Oh my gosh, hon, welcome to your new stage in growing up!' Then, sit her down, take her hands, look into those beautiful eyes (with excitement), and say, 'Are you ready?'

"This is when Rylie is ready to grasp the difference between understanding the little child's Santa and the Spirit of Christmas and how we can pass this divine love onto others. Talk about the phase she went through knowing Santa her first four or five years, which brought awe and excitement when receiving presents, and then learning about Old St. Nick at six or seven, Jesus's birth, the little drummer boy, and the three wise men.

"Your message to Rylie then is that Christmas is real and this Spirit lives in our hearts. So as we get older, we, too, can take the time to help and give to others so they can feel the joy in their hearts as well. Even buying toys with our own money and giving them to other children who don't have any is a memorable way to share the love and kindness in our hearts.

"For our children to accept change, they must see that we do. In this case, Rylie will pay close attention to how you and your husband present this add-on, this new branch to the only concept of Christmas she has ever known. And as she understands—'Ah...this is a part of growing up, like riding a bike when I was ready and when I learned that my teachers don't live at school and wait for us to return each day'—she will also grasp that the world does not stop at the end of her town. It is round and VERY, VERY BIG! Then, she will adjust accordingly and see these changes as nothing to be sad or afraid of but of challenges to grow by. The older she gets, the more she will understand how this world works together and how her gifts will help others on their journey.

"So in the meantime, seeing this transition coming, plan for some unforgettable memories that she will look back on with joy, and most likely, if she has children of her own, those memories will be spoken about each Christmas, and she will do the same because of it."

Cheryl's response was, "Christmas gets hectic, and people forget why we celebrate it because it all becomes about the stuff. Thank you for sharing this perspective. I will save this and share it in conversations with those with the same concerns as their children begin to transition into their next life phase. Honestly, this needs to be kept and read, and perhaps being a homeroom parent, I can share it with her class when they are older!"

"Wonderful," I said, and the spirit of Christmas continues!

Photo by Myriam Zilles on Unsplash

Thought to ponder:

When did you realize the Santa Claus you knew growing up shifted into Santa's Spirit, and how did you embrace it?

21

Valentine's Day Poem

To celebrate Valentine's Day, I've written a poem to honor this day delightfully and playfully.

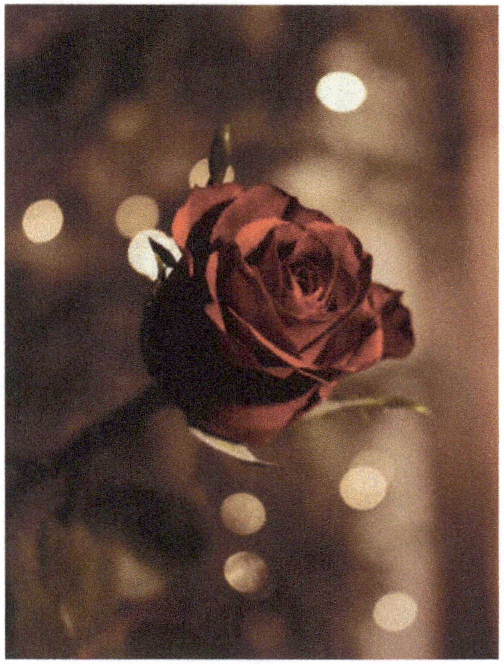

Jamie Street on Unsplash

It is essential to remember the word *love* symbolizes the awesome energy surrounding us constantly in any genre we decide to use to bring awareness of our understanding of It. Enjoy!

A Valentine Rendezvous

Sharing a glance from across the
    table, their eyes twinkling.
He gets up, moves closer, and offers his hand.
She accepts, and they gracefully glide
    across the room to dance.
Music softly plays as he gently pulls her
    close, their energy melts together.

Lights dim, music moves their arms to
    embrace, and they tenderly kiss.
Through a moment's glance, passion
    rises, calling to be fed.
Sensing desire in the closeness of their
    breath, they kiss once more.
The music ceases, reaching for each other's
    hands, they slowly leave the dance floor.

Keys slide the door open as heels lead the way.
Smooth lips lightly brush the skin
    igniting the swirling passion.
Love unlocks the space where desire,
    passion, and closeness unite.
Sheets tangled, candles flicker, bodies embrace,
    the heat intensifies, and Love erupts.

Warmth engulfs them; they breathe in
    and exhale into tranquility.
The evening mist softly dissolves on their
    skin, and in stillness one whispers,

"The eyes that first explored my heart forty
years ago still powerfully ignites me."
A gentle finger moves on warm skin,
acknowledging this truth.

They float away into dreams,
Of what Love was,
And the continuation of what Love is,
Forever and a day.

Thought to ponder:
What kind of love ignites you to float away into dreams?

22

"Open Up Your Eyes. I Am a Blessing in Disguise. (Young Jeezy)"

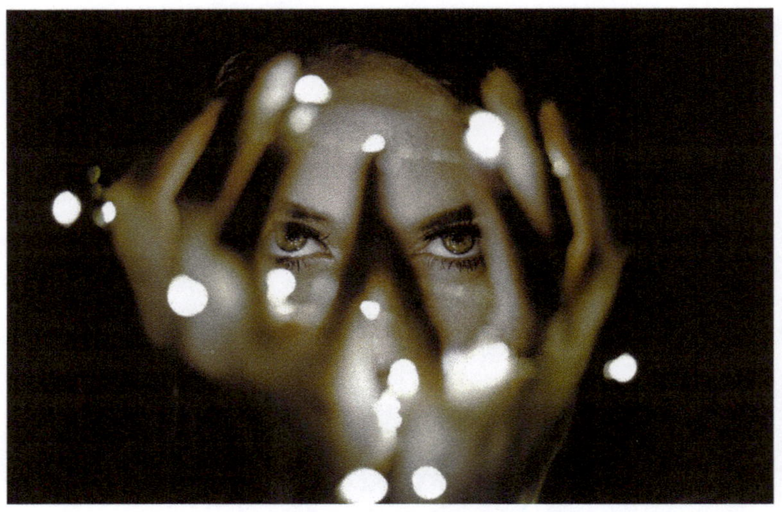

Photo by Rhett Wesley on Unsplash

Marje and I go way back from when our now-adult children were small and in the same schools. We worked as lunch-duty moms and teacher assistants and shared the same trailer to correct papers. We spent many mornings laughing at the craziness of our family life.

There was never a dull moment with her six children and my four. She was barely 5'5", but her solid Scottish accent and always-in-control attitude, combined with a dash of dry humor, made her seem at least six feet tall! (She thought wearing short heels all the time added to her height!)

As the years went by and our children grew, we worked together in the same office. I was a youth minister, and Marje was our secretary. She ran that place like nobody's business. We all knew who was in charge, and we were grateful. Marje was about fifteen years older and was good at listening to friends' woes. She had a way of making problems seem not so overwhelming. We'd sit out back on our breaks, she'd light up a cigarette or two with a hot cup of tea, and the wisdom that came out of her left us feeling pretty uplifted when we returned to work.

We were friends who worked, traveled, cried, laughed, and went through many challenging experiences together. Until…

The separation

I was going to marry someone from my past before I knew Marje. He had stepped back on my path, and because he lived in another state, we'd marry in my hometown and then move across the country. She disapproved. She didn't know him and became very protective, like a mother, not a friend. She said she'd give the marriage six months tops. And because of not seeing eye to eye on this new path, she did not come to the wedding, nor some of our friends that stood by her side with this attitude, and we ended up parting on very unhealthy terms.

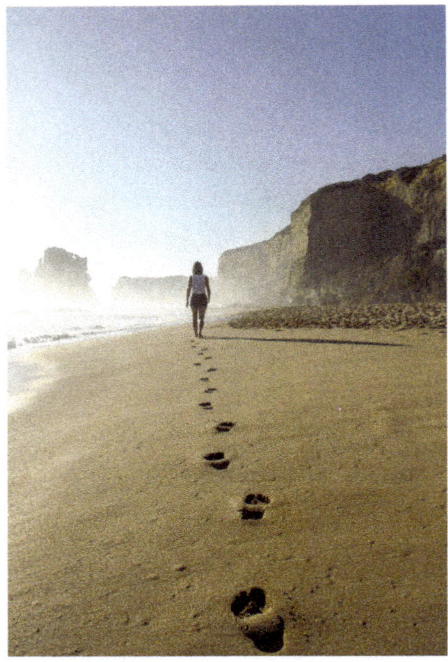

Photo by Brian Mann on Unsplash

During those years, it was tough for me. My mom had passed away two weeks after I married, and my best friend wanted nothing to do with me. So I would write in my journal asking the Spirit to help me be at peace with this separation, and I would send only positive love her way every day. This lightened the heart of the heaviness her absence brought to my life.

I told my husband a funny story about Marje over dinner a few years later. Afterward, he asked if I thought maybe it was time to give her a call. "After all," he said, "it has been five years, and I can see how much you miss her."

I made excuses why I shouldn't call. "She might hang up on me," or "The lies she said about you are still hard for me to swallow." Deep inside, I knew, though, that if she rejected me again, emotionally, I'd be a mess. My husband reassured me if she did not want to talk, I'd know then to bring closure to the relationship and he would be there to help me through it.

The call

When Marje answered the phone with that beautiful Scottish accent, my heart sank. I realized then how much I had missed her, and I could also hear the joy in her voice. When she asked how I was, in my best Scottish accent, I said, "Ah, Marjorie, I've been missing ya something awful!" She laughed. It was music to my ears to hear her laugh again, and we ended up talking for two hours, making plans for me to come to visit.

I found at that moment, when I genuinely released my anger and frustrations to Spirit of what happened five years earlier, my heart felt lightened and at peace. It was more important for me to reconnect with my close friend than to be right about the things that brought the division in the first place.

The visit

Three weeks later, as I flew into one of the smallest airports I had ever seen, I could actually see her van waiting out front. Even though she and her husband had moved to another state, I felt like I was coming home. I couldn't wait!

The second night there, we stayed up until 4:00 a.m., sifting through the anger, what was said and unsaid, and all the questions and hurts of five years ago, everything. It was a cleansing experience for us, and the rest of the week was perfect.

She worked at an after-school program, and I'd go with her, play with the kids, and get them all riled, just to get her goat. Another day, she made my favorite shortbread cookies, and I made her lemon meringue pie. We then made a pot of tea, and both just about finished our desserts in one sitting, not even paying attention as we shared laughs from our past.

As we said our goodbyes, we hugged, and Marje said in that accent of hers, "No more tears, Ter. Everything is fine now, and I'll make my road-trip plans to your place in a few weeks to get to know that man of yours." So I left, thanking Spirit for hearing my prayers, and my heart was indeed at peace.

The unexpected news

Two weeks after my visit, I got a call one evening that Marje had died of a massive heart attack while leaving work that day. After my breath returned to my lungs, I could only close my eyes and thank Spirit, remembering the conversation Marje, her son, and I had on the last night I was there.

After all this time away, Marje's son had mentioned how odd it was that I was there in their home, laughing and sharing like old times. It seemed to him like serendipity in the works. But I told him, "To me, it was more like 'God's grace,' that Spirit knew how hard it had been on your mother and me (I winked at her), and it was time to bring our hearts back together because life was way too short not to!"

This blessing in disguise unfolded itself right in front of me before I could even see it.

I had to smile gratefully to Spirit for finding one of my most precious relationships so essential that It made sure we reconciled before her passing.

This experience also showed me that even though I am just one heart in this incredible, sometimes overwhelming big world, Spirit lives within us, no exceptions, listening and mending our hearts in ways only It can. And it is our choice whether to acknowledge this divine interaction or not. I chose interaction and continue to do so each moment of my life.

Photo courtesy of Pixabay

The takeaway gift

I wrote this story many years ago, but the lesson received has no expiration date and can be found throughout all our lives. Sometimes, doors must be physically closed to protect ourselves, but forgiveness within is essential for allowing peace to open the door and make a home again in our hearts.

Thought to ponder:

What door has closed for you that you might reopen and make a home again in your heart?

23

"Try as Hard as You Will. You Cannot Hold the World from Changing. (Aaron, Quote from om@deepspring.org)"

Courtesy of https://pixabay.com

Every morning, I receive a few positive reflections from different sources to ponder. It brings me to a place of balance as I step out the door to experience a new day.

Today's reflection is from Deep Spring Center. It is a site for meditation and spiritual inquiry. Their wisdom teachings guide us to live with increasing wisdom, compassion, and an open heart.

Today's reflection deeply resonated with me, and I am passing its wisdom on to you. Have a beautiful, *present*, thoughtful day.

Daily reflection~

> Try as hard as you will, you cannot hold the world from changing.
>
> You cannot hold other people or yourself from changing.
>
> To try to do that with yourself so as to please another is unloving to yourself, asking yourself not to be true to yourself and your experience.
>
> It's also unloving to another because it gives them a false hope that you are as they may try to make you to be.
>
> The greatest gift you can give is the willingness to have enough love and respect for another not to live your life around their fear.

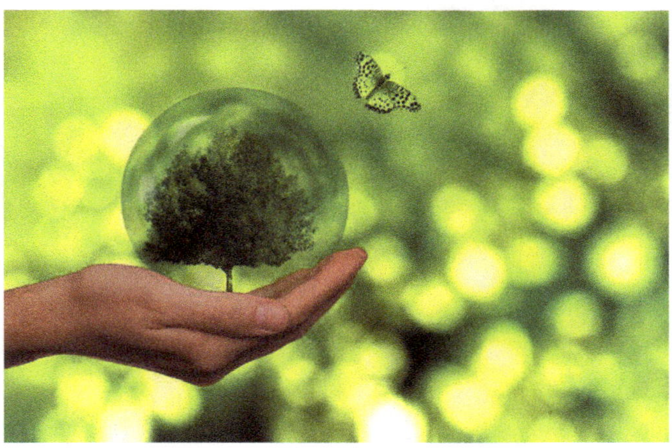

Courtesy of https://pixabay.com

Thought to ponder:

My takeaway from this quote is that by staying true to who I am, will change the world on its own. And yours?

24

A Common Word That Can Impact Our Health

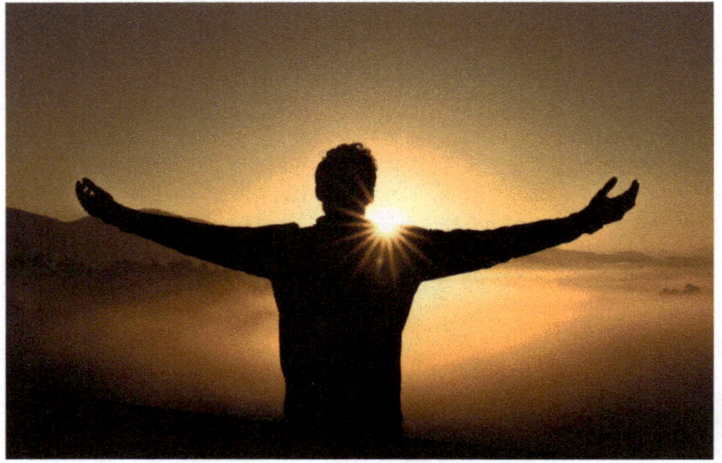

Photo by Zac Durant on Unsplash

Have you ever paid attention to how your body reacts when using certain words?

Well, over the years, there is one word I have worked very hard on giving up, and whoa, what a huge difference it has made! So I wanted to pass on a few things I've learned about this word your way.

The word is *hate*.

It is such a strong word that when using it in a sentence, like "I hate the taste of onions," it can force the upper body to lunge forward ever so slightly that we don't even know it. When saying the sentence this way, "I dislike the taste of onions," or "I don't care for onions," the upper body doesn't move or react.

Now, using the word *hate* in a stronger statement, like "I hate when people show up late for meetings," or "I hate flies. They are everywhere in the summer," the body responds again with that quiet lunge. It's as though the cells are moving in a quick sort of fight mode with a chaotic edge, and agitation sets in.

Then, if we were to change the sentence to "I don't like when people show up late for a meeting. It's just inconsiderate," or "Flies can be so annoying…they're everywhere in the summer," there is a difference in the response from the body, no lunging.

A few years back, I went to a Caroline Myss workshop. She has been around since the early 1970s and is a medical intuitive and a gifted speaker. Her expertise is in human consciousness, spirituality, mysticism, health, energy medicine, and the science of medical intuition. She has written many books on these topics, and the one that stands out for me now is *Anatomy of the Spirit*. She dives into how the body and the Spirit work together or not and the issues we carry that block the alignment of the two.

When I was at the workshop, she spoke about the power of our words. Then, we experimented with using different words and their effects on our bodies, which intrigued me enough to start tuning in to my own words and the dialogue I used every day, to use more positive words in expressing myself, not only with others but also with myself.

The transformation for me has been profound.

When I started experimenting with this word on my own, I was intrigued by how the body reacted and how my senses would perk up depending on how intensely I'd use the term. So I thought of a sentence that really pushed my buttons and said it out loud with solid conviction. "I am consumed with hate for people who couldn't care less about working when they are fully able and use others to give them handouts!" And then I would think about the times I've seen this happening, and my blood would start boiling.

My body would then go through stages of erratic feelings. First, the eyebrows would squint; then, heat would start rising from my feet, up to the chest to the face, and the breath would shorten. Finally, the cells inside me felt like they were on fire, bringing the body to a place of being off-balance and extremely uncomfortable.

When I'd see groups of people protesting about something and on the other side of the street, those who disagreed were protesting too, I'd step back a minute and watch. From the expressions on their faces, hands, and voices on both sides, it was evident that the anger on both sides had the same energy.

I saw with new eyes and thought, *What is being accomplished here? This kind of energy is morphing into a massive ball of negativity that is growing into a destructive kind of hell! Whoa!*

The more I watched, the more my body had the same chaotic reaction; it was scary.

I realized then that when I used the word *hate* or heard someone else use it, the cells in my body would instantly begin to stand up on high alert, like it was preparing for battle, again with a chaotic edge to defend and to protect. I concluded that the body listens to every word we use, how we use it, and how our mind articulates it and then responds accordingly.

Photo by Kira auf der Heide on Unsplash

Hate is used so often and mindlessly that it has become commonplace. How our cells respond to this word should tell us how important it is to use it sparingly or, better yet, not at all.

A positive change in thinking and our words can produce a healthier, lighter body. When we intentionally do this, our cells can continue their work in a more focused and relaxed way without jumping into high alert, putting on their fighting gear, and wasting a lot of energy to protect us when there's no need.

Thought to ponder:

Here's a challenge for the next couple of days—observe the way words are used wherever you are. Then, listen closely to what people are saying, and see how your body reacts. Is it negative or positive? Your body's response will let you know.

Please remember that we have the power to direct our bodies into chaos or peace. It is our choice and only our choice. For the health of our minds, bodies, and hearts, it's worth a try, no?

25

The Day My Heart Fainted

Pexels/Klaus Nielsen

When I left the hospital forty-five years ago without my newborn baby, I could not speak.

Moments before, when I quietly slipped to the nursery window to say goodbye and saw the empty crib, my body filled with numbness, and my heart fainted.

I walked away dazed.

The next thing I knew, I was being wheeled out to my mother's car with flowers in my lap and no baby. I whispered a thank you to the orderly as she helped me into the car and said no more.

As we drove home, Mom asked if I was okay. I shook my head with a yes as tears fell.

As I rested that afternoon, my heart woke up, and I could sense her listening for the sounds of our new baby. But she was confused because all she felt was a deep, painful emptiness, I felt her start to bleed, and she fainted again.

Mom left for work early the following day, and my siblings went to school. Our little dog of ten years lay quietly by my side. I could tell he knew something was wrong by the little whimpers he released between his breaths.

Once alone, I awakened my heart and softly told her the whole story, hoping she would understand. But instead, the pillow wrapped around my stomach stifled the heart's scream when she realized what I had done.

My throat tightened as I called out to Spirit in desperation. I was begging to be comforted, held, rocked, or anything to soothe this deep wound. Was I being heard? I didn't know; I couldn't even listen to myself over the heart's constant wailing.

I tried to calm her down, but she would have none of it. We were both out of control, and all my pup could do was cry with us.

I stopped, breathed deep, and folded myself into a tight ball, rocking myself, and with barely a voice left, I whispered, "Please, Spirit, I need You here to reassure me that I did the right thing. This baby, my baby, deserves so much. All I have to offer is my love; this could not feed or clothe this little one. I work at a fast-food restaurant, live at home, and have no money, and this is not a healthy way to raise a child."

Crying softly into my knees, I felt a stillness, a silence, and my heart fainted again.

A few minutes later, the doorbell rang, followed by knocking. I wiped my eyes, quickly wiped my nose, and went to the door. There was my brother's girlfriend, Angela, looking at me with eyes of compassion.

I could not speak; all I could do was look at her.

"Terry, I was in the neighborhood and wanted to stop by to see how you were doing. Are you okay?" I fell to my knees, and the tears I held back fell all over the floor. She then moved to the floor, wrapped her arms around me, and soothingly said the words I desperately needed to hear, "You made the right decision. Please believe this. Your baby will be cared for and loved so deeply. You don't have to worry." As I listened to her words, I heard only Spirit surrounding me, comforting me in a love that overpowered me into calmness.

After Angela left, I lay on the bed, eyes closed, focusing on my heart. Did she wake up? Is she okay? I waited to feel some stirring, a lightness, but there was only silence. It had been an emotional day for both of us; rest was required for healing, so I humbly gave her that space.

It was also time for me to take a few deep breaths, rest, and be grateful for this moment. Spirit had heard my plea and genuinely came forward through this angel (Angela was her name) to reassure me that my child would be treasured and I had given a precious selfless gift to a couple who will always cherish this divine new life.

It was then—at that moment—I felt peace.

Thought to ponder:

When we truly ask for guidance, reassurances, and comfort from Spirit, if we pay attention, we'll experience it, as in this case with my brother's girlfriend, Angela. It could have been any of my friends or family who came to the door that day, but it was Angela. Spirit made sure, without a shadow of doubt, that my desperate call was answered by sending an Angel(a) to comfort me.

When has your call for help been answered, and how did you know?

26

Do We Really Matter in This World?

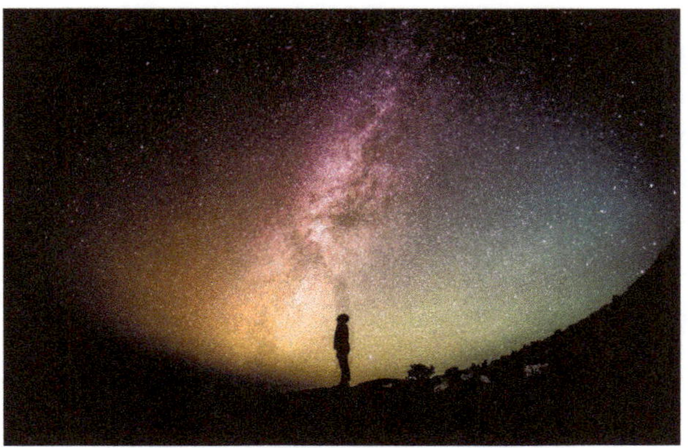

Photo by Greg Rakozy on Unsplash

I just came in from a quiet moment with nature. The stillness was beautiful. Walking down to the water, among the grasses, tiny white flowers were sporadically spread about. They seem to be standing strong as if to say, "Don't step on me. I am important, and it matters that I am here!" So I made sure my steps respected their space.

As I sat on the dock, the evening mist traveled almost breathlessly over the water like a transparent screen. I could only see it if I focused, and it too seemed to be calling out. "Without me, this scene would not be complete. It matters that I am here!"

Looking into the water, at first, the depth could not be seen because of the darkness it carried. As I focused though, a small fish was swimming around the ladder secured to the dock. Just watching it move made me smile, because there was a fishing boat a little farther out and maybe the fish felt safe staying closer to shore. As the moments passed, and I stayed focused, I began to see fish of all sizes swimming near me. I wondered if they thought they mattered.

Walking back up to the house, I stopped at the base of a huge pine tree, whose trunk I focused on. I was amazed at the strength of its bark and the thickness of its roots, just standing there in all of its magnificence, not asking anyone to take notice. It doesn't have to, for it is respected just because of what it is!

The mighty pine doesn't have to worry whether it matters, as its stance on earth is deeply rooted. As I focused on this tree, it focused back. The energy between us was felt. I put my hands on it for a moment and thanked it for being here and for what it has taught me, to be aware of the importance of stillness, to allow the friction of the world to move past me like the wind without fear, and to trust that the stability of my roots are anchored with calming sturdiness.

The beauty of Spirit's imagination is full of awe and so powerful to me.

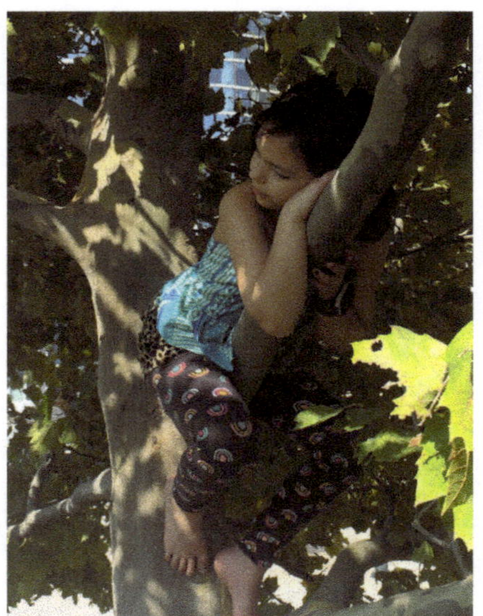

Photo by John P. Salvatore

I tell my bones, "You are my roots, and we have this kind of strength too. Stay courageous." Then, I reminded myself that I was created with this same awe and to not forget to take the time to be still, and reflect on this birthright, because it is truly who I am.

Walking up the wooden stairs to our deck, tears slowly streamed down my face. No doubt responding to the way nature was communicating with me but also in gratitude to our Creator for showing itself so clearly and understanding that to know I mattered, right now, in this world, was important to me. This energy was profoundly felt.

I really wanted to share this deep internal stirring. I don't know why. Maybe because I had just read another chapter in *Radical Acceptance*, by Tara Brach. She had stated, "We experience our lives through our bodies whether we are aware of it or not." And in that moment, I paused, took a deep breath, and could feel an alignment—the awareness of this earthly connection took hold.

That's when I had to put the book down because the emotions took the reins, and it was as if the words were speaking directly to me.

The walk outside was rejuvenating.

When deep emotions seem to move up and want to be released, it is so important to allow them this freedom because it clears the way for openness, the calmness, and the stillness, which we all need.

For me, after a strong release of stuck energy and emotions and a few deep breaths, there is a renewed awareness, like fog on a mirror after a hot shower, and the glass slowly dissipates and reflects its surroundings clearly.

Eventually I shared these feelings with a wonderful friend, and after listening, her suggestion was a simple mantra: "Breathing in…I am home. Breathing out…I have arrived."

When I began to fall asleep at night and again before getting out of bed in the morning, I would focus on breathing, and these words. Over time, I found that the deeper I breathed in, the more clarity seeped in. When I exhaled slowly and completely, it was as though the strength of that mighty pine tree had grounded itself firmly within me.

Thought to ponder:

If we quiet ourselves, breathe, and focus on who we are as a person, the knowing is there. We are *all* connected, remembering that we have the power to touch hearts just by an authentic smile or a warm hug, by encouraging someone who can't see their own strength, or even by pulling a chuckle out of a situation that was getting heavy and going nowhere. In those moments, we will soften and realize that we do indeed matter in this world and it is a kinder place because we are here, and that matters!

27

Connecting through Mental Illness

"This is only my body, Mom, not me. I am standing next to you and am fine."

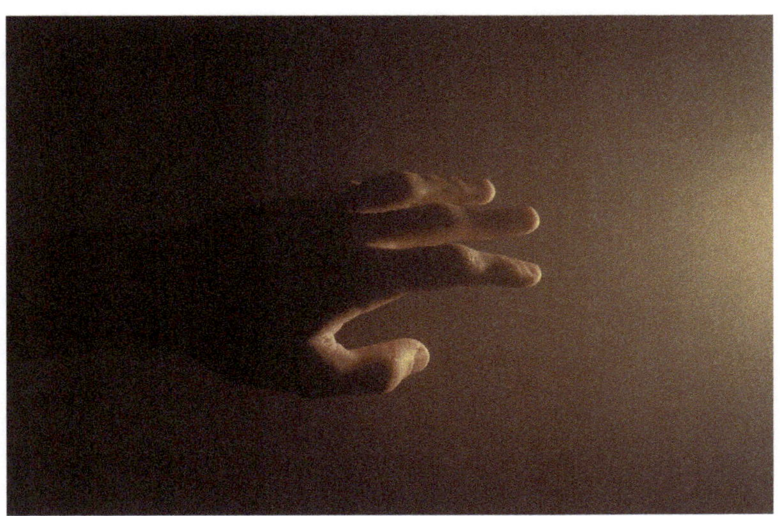

Photo by Jackson David on Unsplash

I was married in February 1979 to a man who had two-year-old twin boys, Bobby and his brother, from his first marriage. Because of circumstances, the twins did not see or speak with their biological mother until they became teenagers. Over the next five years, we had two more boys together.

After a strenuous fifteen-year marriage, we divorced. The twins, now in high school, moved with their father a few miles away, and the younger boys stayed with me. At their dad's insistence, I had very little interaction with the twins, although word around town was that they started hanging around with the tough kids and later dabbled in drugs and alcohol. Bobby had strange reactions to the drugs he experimented with, even after they wore off.

When Bobby was young, he had problems with sweaty palms, anxiety, and the need to be perfect, from his hair to his clothes. It wasn't an ego thing; it was simply a pattern of keeping everything in order. And for Bobby, when it wasn't, the anxiety became overwhelming. We didn't overthink it then; we just thought it was part of growing up. However, by his late teens, the anxiety and paranoia became so intense that he went in for a complete neurology exam. He was diagnosed with schizophrenia, and his drug usage accelerated the onset of the disorder. He was eighteen years old.

The next four years were very difficult for all of us. So many diagnosed with schizophrenia feel incredibly uncomfortable in closed places. It was no different with Bobby, and the streets became his haven.

I'd be driving around town and see him walking barefoot, arms stretched out, talking to no one. Emotions would bombard me from all directions at the same time.

"I've got to stop!"

"No, I can't stop; I don't know if his reaction would be controllable!"

"No, I have to…but…Bobby, I don't know what to do!"

Tears would flow, and I felt the strong urge to throw up!

I'd make it through the front door just in time to lose control, fall apart, and end up huddled in the corner of the house, hugging my legs, and saying repeatedly, "Bobby, honey, I am so sorry!"

One day, when I came home from work, I glanced through the window next to the front door and saw both younger boys (now ten and fourteen) just sitting on the couch. There was no TV or radio blasting as usual, and they had very fearful looks on their faces. Then, when I entered the house, I could see the whole couch.

"What's going on, kids?" I asked, shutting the door behind me.

Before they could answer, Bobby turned around and said, "Hi, Mom! I was talking to the boys."

Without missing a beat, I said, "Hey, sweetie. Boys, I'm sure you have homework to do."

I didn't have to say it twice, and they were gone.

Bob followed me into the kitchen.

"Hon, you know the rules. You are welcome in this house but only when I am here."

"I guess I forgot. Hey, Mom, I wanted to talk to you."

"Okay, let's talk," and we sat down at the kitchen table.

I don't remember a lot about that conversation, but I remember him explaining that he had ridden his bike ten miles to see me and asked if I could give him a ride home.

His father had told me to be careful around Bobby. He could change his personality anytime, become dangerous, and possibly harm me. I wasn't concerned with that at all. The physical pain he could inflict was nothing compared to the pain my heart carried every day. If he came after me physically, there was no fear. I would handle it.

So I packed his bike in the trunk and took him to the apartment he shared with a friend. He did most of the talking, telling me he would try out for baseball and make it big one day. It made me smile. He sounded joyful for just a few moments, and his humor lightened my sadness. We hugged as he took his bike and headed for his apartment.

A couple of days later, Bobby was arrested for preaching the Bible on his balcony at 2:00 a.m. He was taken to a rehab center and placed in lockdown about twenty miles from our home.

This behavior became Bobby's new normal. He would float in and out of my life. He was back in rehab six months later, and I felt it was essential to see him. He had been in this overcrowded facility a few times before but prior to this was released on good behavior and promised to take his medicine.

Visitors to the facility had to pass through three separate doors, each made of thick metal and locks that echoed as they slammed every time someone passed through. We had to leave all our belongings outside the first door and would collect them on the way out.

Bobby rarely took his medicine, making him feel sluggish and very tired. When he was at the center and given medication, he would hide it under his tongue and then slip it into his pocket when they left. He was irrational and unpredictable, and the facility had no other option but to keep him locked in his room when not supervised.

The first time I went to see him, he was sleeping. They didn't allow me to enter his room as they couldn't guarantee Bobby's reaction and my safety. However, there was a rectangular window on the door that I could look through. The security guard welcomed me to stay as long as I wanted and said that if Bobby woke up, to let him know and he'd bring him out.

The room had one piece of furniture, a bed with a thin mattress. Bobby's shoes lay on the floor next to the wall. They were tattered and worn with no shoelaces just in case he got creative and tried to harm himself with them. His Bible lay next to him. The cover was black and the material worn. Bobby used the words to preach to others the easy access to hell if they did not follow the road to righteousness.

As I examined this young man, I found him to be peaceful. His hair was unwashed and past his shoulders, and the greasiness took on a shiny glow, giving him a somewhat dignified look. The clothes were simple and stained. His feet were the color of sand, as if he had been trekking through the desert for days.

My eyes moved again to his face. How many times did I wash that face and kiss those cheeks?

When he was younger, I remember him telling me, "Mom, I'm going to be a basketball star when I grow up!"

We always thought he'd be a bank president. Even as a young man, he had carried himself with a sophisticated, suave kind of charm. Just looking into his deep brown Italian eyes, you were hooked!

And funny? He was hilarious!

I remember walking into the kitchen once and seeing him washing the dishes with wads of tissue stuffed up his nose.

"Bob? Really?"

"Mom, this is the best way to stop my nose from running, and it works!" Then he'd do a little dance around the trash can.

"How you make me laugh, honey!"

As my focus returned to the window, looking through to my son's withering body, my eyes filled with painful tears of what was and what is now. I knew I couldn't stay.

A few more months passed, Bobby was back in rehab, and his mindset was further out of control. He was now hearing angry voices and more forceful in his desire to save people from going to hell. He felt it was his calling. And for some reason, the book of Revelations brought him so much fear; that was all he talked about.

The rehab center was losing patience with his outbursts and was almost at their limits with him. His mental stability continued to decline when he talked about taking his life. I didn't care what his father told me; I would see him.

Back at rehab, the last door to the visiting room slammed behind me, and I glanced around the room. The last time I saw Bobby, he had been sleeping, and I chose to let him sleep. This time I spotted him in the middle of the room, pacing with his head down, holding his Bible close, and talking to himself. His hair was still shoulder length and unwashed. His clothes hung on his thin frame, and he was barefoot.

Instantly, I felt a lump in my throat and wanted to cry. It was something my heart always did when I saw him, and this time was no different. I was able to swallow it down and soothed my emotions by saying to myself, "You can do this, Terry. You must do this. He needs to know how much he is loved. Breathe deeply now, and step forward. Your heart will take care of the rest."

Everyone in the room seemed to fade into the walls, and I heard no voices except my own.

"Bobby, honey?"

He turned and faced me. At first, he didn't recognize me. It's like when you see a family member in a place you would never expect them to be, and for a split second, it's like you're looking at them for the first time. But when our eyes met, the connection was made.

"Mom! What are you doing here?" His eyes began to water.

"I came to see you, honey!"

As he came closer, he wrapped one arm around my back, the other clutching the Bible. Then, instinctively, he put his forehead on my shoulder and started to cry.

Quietly Bobby said, "Mom, I've missed you so much…why have you come?"

His ear was close to my lips, and I whispered, "To spend some time with you, sweetheart."

He was crying hard now, and his body began to shake.

I quietly said, "Let's sit down."

It took a few minutes for him to calm down, and as I held and soothed him, I asked God to please let me feel my strength to bring this child some peace, to keep me focused, and to let the tears flow later.

Bobby then looked up at me, eyes deep brown, dilated and red, and so sad. He said, "Mom, I have to ask you something?" He tightened his hand on the Bible. "Was I a good boy when I was little?"

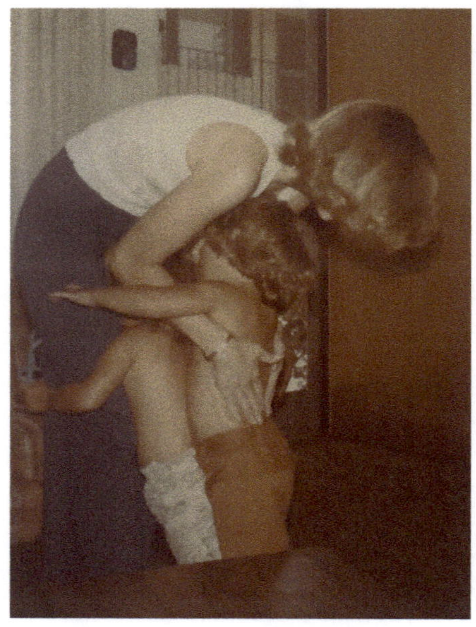

(Photo by the author)

"Of course, you were a very good child and absolutely adorable!"

His face became serious again. "It says in the Bible that the bad will go to hell, and I'm afraid I'm going there. I hear God's voice telling me that's where I'm going! I don't want to go there, Mom!"

His lips began to quiver, and a few tears rolled down his cheek.

I could hear myself clearly inside, *Be strong! Be focused!*

I moved my hands to cup his face. "Look at me, Bobby, and listen very carefully. God did not tell you you were going to hell. He is a God of only love! You hear voices from this disease and from not taking your medicine. It is not God!" I waited for the words to sink in. "Listen to me…I did not give birth to you, right?" He shook his head yes. "But I've raised you and your brother since you were two years old. In my heart, you are and always will be my child. You and your brother are no different from the younger boys." I stopped for a moment and cocked my head to one side and said, "Let's say that these voices were true…which they are not, but let's just say you were to go to hell. Well then, I would go with you."

His eyes lightened.

"I would go with you, protect you, and we would find a way out together. I would never leave you! Do you understand this?"

Again, he moved his head up and down.

"Now, if I carry this much love for you, can you only imagine how much love God carries for you?" Looking into his eyes to make sure our connection was clear, I continued, "It says in the Bible that God is all love, Bobby, and God, being ALL love, would never send you or anyone else to hell. Love doesn't do that!" I gave it a few minutes to sink in and then said, "Honey, have I ever lied to you?"

His eyes became softer as a tear floated on the bottom rim, and he said quietly, "No."

"Then you can believe me now that what I'm saying is the truth. Okay?"

His words broke a little, and he answered, "Okay," and he again lay his head on my shoulder.

"Another thing, hon. If the words in this Bible are scaring you, you do not understand its message. It is not to scare you but to guide you in life. Please stop reading it if that is not what it is doing for you. When was the last time you laughed and enjoyed the sunshine?"

He gave no answer.

"Give your mind a rest, child. Watch a funny movie or read something light, okay?"

Still, there was no answer. I could feel his body relax as I spoke. My voice had always done this for the boys. They didn't listen to my words as much as they would feel soothed by the sound of my voice.

After a few minutes, a bell sounded, and then an announcement came on over the intercom stating visiting time was over and to please start exiting through the main door. Bobby's body jerked as if falling in a dream, and I quietly told him it was time for me to go. Almost whispering, he asked me not to. I responded, "Hon, please remember that I love you and will always love you, no matter what."

The moment was broken when two security guards came over and gently said that visiting time was over. So we stood, and as my son put his arms around me, I could feel his chest shake, he didn't want to let go, and I was afraid for him.

"Bobby, it's time to go," I said and whispered again, "I love you."

He quietly responded, "I love you, Mom."

His hold was tight, and then he looked at me. When our eyes met, there was an unspoken bond. Call it a communion, a familiarity, or an understanding of connection, but it was there and deeply felt.

The guard gently took Bobby's arm, and I could feel him stiffen.

"Go, hon."

He looked deeply into my eyes one more time and then looked down as he was led to his cell. I didn't move until I could no longer see him. The feeling of peace was fading with him, only to be replaced with weakness of the heart. The bubble I was able to swallow and hide in some sacred place throughout our visit slowly returned. Patients and visitors were gone, except for a couple of guards standing around talking and looking my way. I breathed deeply and moved toward the door with my head and body straightened. As I stepped through and it shut, the echo made my shoulders jump. The distance to the second door seemed longer.

I felt weaker, tears started filling behind my eyes, the next door seemed to bang harder as it shut, and I felt my lower lip begin to quiver. And even though I was still walking tall, I could not feel my feet. With my eyes straight ahead, my breathing became shallow.

Wham! Went the third and final door. The noise of the door's lock felt like a gun had been fired and the bullet grazed my left ear as it passed. I don't know how I was able to ask for my belongings or even walk to my car, but I made it.

Once inside the car, I couldn't hold on any longer. Emotions overcame me. I felt tight spasms in my throat, and breathing became difficult. Then, I slowly allowed myself to calm down. *Think about nothing but breathing. Relax your throat, and soften your heart. Calm down. He will be okay. He knows you love him.* As I mentally spoke to myself, I found my own words soothing, and then I just rested my eyes.

A few weeks later, I had made plans to revisit Bobby. I heard the rehab center was so fed up with his outbursts and refusing to take his medication that they literally threw him out the door, along with his Bible. He ran back and banged on the door, begging to let him back in. But they refused.

A week later, on a Sunday afternoon, as I settled in to watch the movie *Ghost*, I got a phone call from a close friend whose son grew up with the boys. She told me that Bobby had run toward a moving trolley downtown, jumped in front of it, was dragged under, and had died. She also said that no one could get ahold of his dad and needed a family member to verify his body.

I was surprised at how calm I was. It was like I had anticipated this call for over a year, and it had finally come. I could hear my heart say, "No more fears, no more confusion, no more watching this beautiful, precious young man, child of my heart, go through torment one moment longer. He is now free!" I took in a deep long breath and allowed peace to flow slowly from my lips.

A friend who was with me at the time of the call came along. I drove, wholly focused and unemotional. I arrived at the trolley tracks. I could see yellow tape surrounding the trolley where the scene happened a distance back. People and police were everywhere.

When I reached the front of the crowd, an officer stopped me, telling me no one was allowed past the yellow tape. I told him I was Bobby's mother. He took my arm and brought me through to the other side.

I glanced over to the trolley where police officers were standing guard as we walked. I could see Bobby's foot lying front side down, with the shoe still intact, but nothing more. I told myself he was no longer in that body, and I remained focused.

While waiting to talk with the person in charge, a policeman next to me quietly said he was sorry about my son. He said he had a couple of teenagers, and one was having a difficult time with drugs, and it was tough. I stared straight ahead; not taking my eyes off the trolley car, I whispered, "Thank you." Tears rolled down my cheeks, but nothing else moved.

His father and twin brother arrived together. His father was uncontrollable and in no shape to identify Bobby's body. He kept running to the trolley, and the police would catch him, return him to us, and ask him to stay until they had finished. He said he would, and then he would run down again as soon as they let go of him. After the third time, I calmly but firmly took his arms to face me. I looked straight into his pain-filled eyes and told him that he did not want to see Bobby. It would be the last picture he would have of him if he did, and that is not what his son would have wanted. I could feel his arms relax. I handed him over to Bobby's brother and asked him to take his father away for a moment.

A young woman police officer then brought over two Polaroid pictures of Bobby's face, which she had taken when they removed the trolley. "Is this your son," stating his full name.

As I looked, his eyes were closed as if he were sleeping. His face was intact. I could see the base of the neck had moved to one side, and the skin on his neck was stretched tight to keep the two pieces from separating. Inside I heard a voice say, "This is only my body, Mom, not me. I am standing next to you, and I am fine."

I answered without looking up, "Yes, this is Bobby's body."

She then wrote his name on the back of the pictures, thanked me, and walked away.

After a few minutes, I saw that his father was calmer. He was talking on the phone, and my other son came over to let me know they would follow the ambulance to the mortuary. We hugged, and I left to go home.

Bobby died on November 23, 1997. He was twenty-two years old.

When someone lives with a disease such as this and then passes the way Bobby did, family members and close friends will say, "If only we could have, would have, or should have done this or that or something to help, this might not have happened." I would see the heaviness of guilt and sadness in their eyes, especially when we all lived in the same town and had a history together. So when I spoke at the eulogy, I brought this up.

"These words of guilt are just wasted energy and bring nothing but a heaviness that weakens the heart." Then I slowly met the eyes of the young adults Bobby grew up with and said, "If sharing Bobby's story can help someone choose a more positive path, this crazy, beautiful, unpredictable world would be a healthier, peaceful place to live."

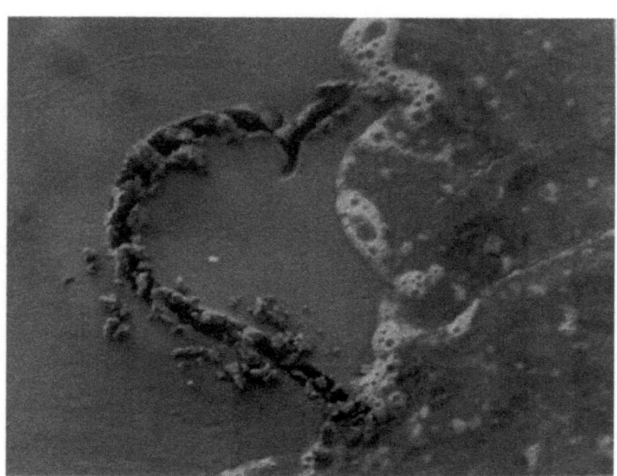

Photo by Gianna Salvatore

Thought to ponder:

What have we learned from our own experiences or from someone else's life that can guide others onto a more positive path?

28

"We Are What We Repeatedly Do. Excellence, therefore, Is Not an Act but a Habit. (Aristotle)"

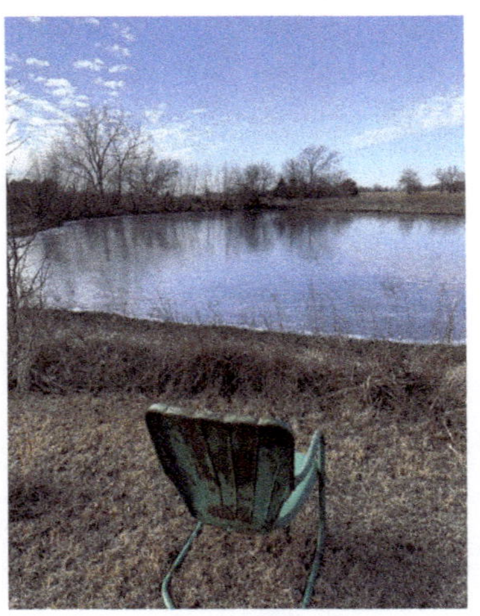

Photographer: John P. Salvatore

I repeatedly breathe,
Therefore, I am alive.
I repeatedly sit in stillness,
Therefore, I am evolving.
I repeatedly enjoy an early morning
cuppa joe as I ponder life,
Therefore, I am loving to myself.

I repeatedly walk in Nature,
Therefore, I am a wanderer.
I repeatedly seek positive energy,
Therefore, I am light.
I repeatedly second-guess myself,
Therefore, I am a perfectionist.
I repeatedly smile at myself in the mirror,
Therefore, reminding myself that I am Love.
I repeatedly read,
Therefore, I am a seeker of wisdom.
I repeatedly write,
Therefore, I am an author.
I repeatedly feed the birds,
Therefore, I am a nurturer.
I repeatedly gravitate to the sun,
Therefore, I am a ray of light.
I repeatedly go within to feel Spirit,
Therefore, I am a creation of Pure Love.
~I Am That I Am.

(Photo by author)

Thought to ponder:
What do you repeatedly do?

29

"Withholding Forgiveness Is like Drinking Poison and Hoping the Other Person Will Die. (Barbara Leger)"

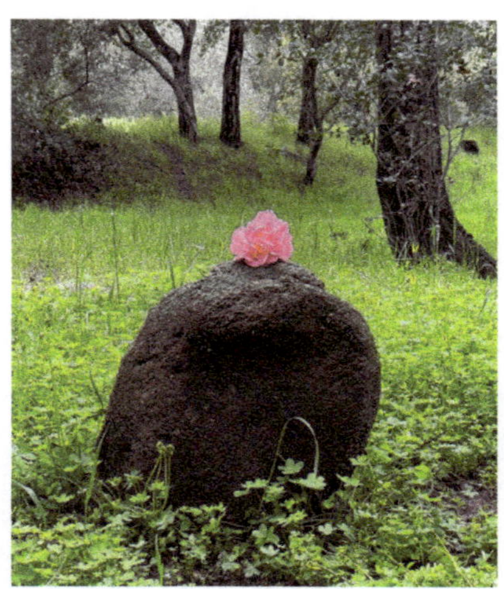

Forgiveness gives us the opportunity to teach from our stories that will change people's direction for the better (photo taken by the author's son while visiting La Cañada Flintridge in Los Angeles)

When I hear someone say, "I will never forgive," there is instant sadness that moves through me.

Yes, a lot is happening in our personal lives and the world that constantly challenges us to forgive. I get this.

Speaking at my son's funeral while looking at the young man sitting in the pew, who supplied him with drugs that enhanced the whirlwind of his mental illness, was more than difficult.

Forgiving those who took the love I carried for them and tossing this precious gift like trash at the age of six, ten, seventeen, twenty-three, and up was continuously an uphill battle.

Reading about and seeing the horrific scenes of this world and in our hometowns has had me clenching my fists and pounding the ground until they bled because there was and is nothing I can do to turn back the hands of time to change what has already happened.

Oh, I get it. Believe me. The human heart and every cell in our bodies shake with anger, disbelief, and tears that could flood the world out of existence.

And yet here we are.

We wake up the following day, and the sun shines, rain falls, snow sparkles, and ocean waves dissolve slowly into the shore. We hear the birds, smell the fresh aroma of the coffee, or feel the warmth of a cup of tea as it moves through our senses.

It is a new day.

What will go on in the world today?

Maybe we will hear about a couple who had tried to have a baby for years and just found out they were pregnant with twins or someone raising money on GoFundMe for the children in his hometown who did not have enough to eat and clothes to wear. He had an accident that put him in a coma that made the news. When he awoke, he found that people had given over a million dollars to his cause. And he wanted to pay it forward. Or someone who has been intensely challenged with alcoholism and was, because of their courage, able to conquer through it with the wisdom to teach others how to do the same.

And maybe, just maybe, as we were preparing for bed, the phone rang from someone who had scarred our hearts many times over, asking for genuine, authentic forgiveness that we thought would never, in a thousand years, happen.

And our hearts began to heal.

Early morning sunrise in Virginia Beach (taken by the author)

Withholding forgiveness takes the essence of what we have to offer ourselves and the world away. When we forgive, space opens and shows us where to make a difference to bring our best to our backyards and communities. Maybe we cannot change what is not ours to change, but we can take our positive energy and spread it around to all that calls to us.

Yes, we can sit in anger and explain why we won't forgive, but the body begins to whither as we do this. The lips turn downward and stick; the body walks with a heaviness that hangs on us like a ball and chain. And our eyes lose their light and creative life, and the world seems more than dark. I have seen and experienced this myself.

And yet here I am.

The good, the holy, and the beautiful live within each of us. When terrible things happen, I believe it is because, for whatever reason, those who do this have blocked their goodness, consciously or unconsciously. Does this mean we are to join them? When we choose not to forgive, we drink the poison, destroying our ability to connect with our true nature. And those who look to us for comfort, reassurance, positivity, and genuine love will lose.

Is this worth it?

I've asked myself this many times, and each time, the beautiful part of me rises, and the light I feel brings the answer. And I quietly smile.

And here I am.

And you who are reading this are here too.

Thought to ponder:

Often, we won't know whose hearts we have touched or the heavy blanket we've uncovered that blocks the love in them. However, Spirit knows, and Its light will do the work to change the world through you and me.

How will you choose to live today, just today, to make a positive difference?

30

It's All about Me

Picture courtesy of Pixabay

As you live deeper in the heart, the mirror gets clearer and cleaner.

—Rumi

It's all about me, you know. Honestly, it is!

Being on vacation years back, my husband and I stumbled onto a sweet little beach store. We're always hoping to find little treasures to take back. So he went in one direction and I in another.

I was sifting through a spring clothing rack when I came upon a T-shirt that said on the front, "It's all about me!" I thought, *Really?*

Who, in their right mind, would wear a shirt like that? How egotistical! "It's all about me!" Right. And I moved on to the next shirt. I stepped to the next rack, still shaking my head.

It's all about me. Why would someone even think about putting a quote like that on a shirt, let alone wear it? Man, people amaze me.

A few racks later, annoyance was getting the better of me. *It's all about me.* Dang. I returned to the shirt and pulled it out to see if I had missed something in that four-word sentence. Maybe I read it wrong. *It's all about me.* Nope, it still said the same thing. Geez, that is so not right.

"And why am I still staring at it? Who cares? You'd never wear a shirt like that. Let it go, and move on." Fine, now I'm arguing with myself. Great.

As I slipped the shirt back into its space, I strolled away. Looking at some pants, here comes the phrase again, "It's all about me." What does *it's* mean anyway? A thought floated past my mind's eye; it's all about you and how you treat others.

Wait, what?

It's about how you care for yourself so you can play with your grandchildren and live a healthier life.

Really? Okay, what else?

It's all about you and how you respect the Earth by not throwing garbage on it and picking up the trash you see on your path. Ahh! Hey! I may be onto something here. It could be all about me by how I listen to others, treat others, share my experiences, and help others see the good in themselves. It could also mean stepping out each day and being the best version of myself.

Oh, wow! This is good; this is really good!

As I turned around to go back to that shirt for the third time, I bumped into my husband. "Find any treasures?" he asked.

"Oh my gosh, I think so. Come look." I pulled the shirt off the rack and put it in front of me.

"Very nice!" he said as a smile moved across his face as in, "That'll look great on you!"

"Very nice? Did you read the quote?"

"Oh, no, I was just thinking it would look great on you." (I knew it!)

"Read it, please."

"It's All About Me. Okay, I got it. Are you going to buy it?" There's that smile again, sheesh.

"Okay, would you focus here…ask me WHY it's all about me?" He looked at me blankly. I rolled my eyes and tapped my foot.

"Okay, okay. Why is it all about you, Terry?"

"Well, thanks for asking. It's all about how I treat, care for, and love myself. It's all about how I honor and respect our relationship and allow us our space together and apart—the way I take care of the Earth, interact with the grandchildren, and love our kids, friends, and people in general. It IS all about me and how I live in the world, which could make a huge difference every moment of every day."

"Whoa, that's pretty deep, but it does make sense. Do you think people will get it as they walk by and read it?" he questioned.

"That's the great thing," I said. "If people ask me, I can casually tell them what I told you. Then, as I did, they can come away with a different perspective from when they first read it. Exciting huh? I can't wait to put it on and try this experiment. Okay, I'm ready to go," moving to the register.

My husband was surprised and said, "You're done? That's it?"

"Yep, I got my message. I'm done here."

A few months later, one of my sons and his then-wife went on vacation with us. He was still in medical school and was up very early. In one of my other stories, titled "Don't Blink," I mentioned as a teen he was NOT a morning person, and it wasn't pretty to be around him then, so I said, "Good morning, hon? What are you doing up?"

Very sweetly, he said, "Oh, I'm a morning person now, Mom. Good morning."

My jaw dropped, and so did my mouth. I quickly covered it. I felt light-headed and thought I was going to faint. I was going into shock and grabbed onto the door frame. (Good thing, he was studying to be a doctor because if I fell and cracked my head. I was in good hands.)

"You okay, Mom? Oh and hey, cool shirt."

I looked down at my shirt, *It's All About Me*. I forgot I had put this shirt on.

"Oh, umm…thanks." I stuttered.

He reads it slowly out loud. "It's All About Me. Uh-huh…interesting." It's his nice way of saying, "I don't get why you're wearing that."

As I gained my composure, I said, "Go ahead, ask me WHY it's all about me."

"Okay, I'll bite. Why is it ALL about you, Mom?"

And I gave him my spiel.

Again, I hear "Uh-huh…interesting. Deep stuff," and he went back to his book.

A few minutes later, his wife walked in, with a coffee cup in hand. "Morning!" She looked at my shirt, read it, and said, "Well, isn't that interesting?"

My son looked up from his book, shook his head no, and said, "Don't ask her WHY." Grrrrr. The cuteness of earlier disappeared, and the brat from years ago came back—ah, the memories.

That shirt is long gone. Though the quote still floats in and out of my wisdom file within. Maybe it's because it is something worth remembering and sharing.

As I walked in thirty-degree weather this morning, the story returned, and the laughter, as I revisited those moments, those feelings warmed me up inside. And after four miles, I convinced myself you all would get it too and could see through my heart the importance of this piece.

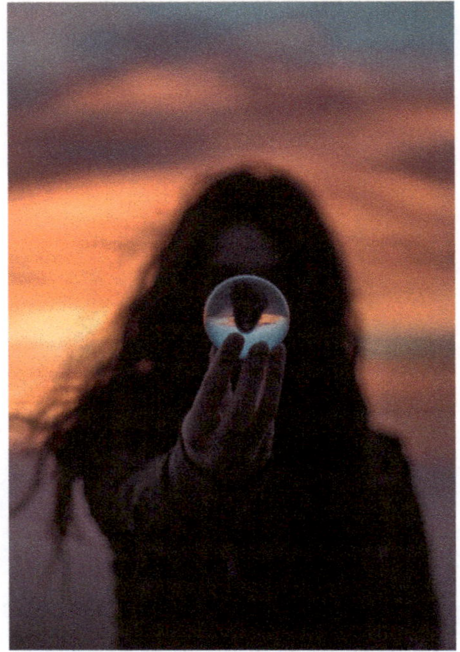

Photo by Garidy Sanders on Unsplash

Final thought to ponder:
If it's not all about you, then who is it about?

ABOUT THE AUTHOR

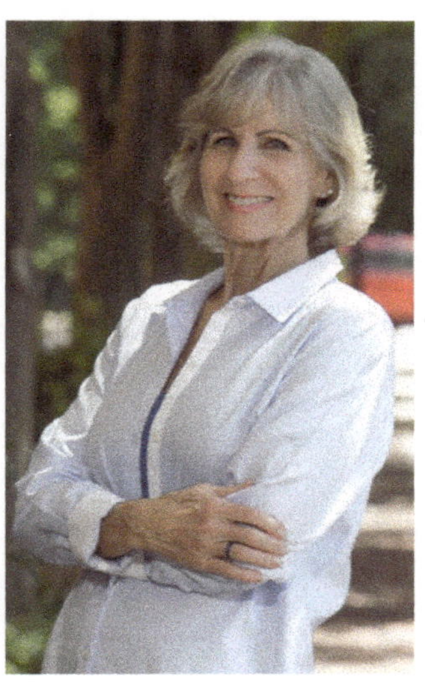

Terese Neely Pottinger is an author residing with her husband in McCormick, South Carolina.

Her purpose is to shine her light, enabling others to discover their paths. For a long time, though, she resisted this calling.

Once she understood that God is not the judgmental being she was raised with but is ALL LOVE, it inspired her to explore spirituality in a more authentic, broader context.

She began studying and practicing yoga and meditation. They aligned with her belief that we are all connected, people, nature, and the universe.

In October 2021, she learned about Medium, a website for writers, and how people of all ages made genuine connections through their writing. So in January 2022, after reading many stories, she published her first one titled, *Cancer: A Positive Teacher.*

Today, she is part of a community of writers on Medium. She shares the wealth of personal stories she's written over the years and responds to others whose stories connect with the truth of who she is. They are like-minded people sharing sincerity and honesty through their writings. They honor each other's work in gratitude and genuine support.

This book represents a collection of personal stories, pulled from Medium, that significantly shaped who she is today.

If you'd like to know more about Medium or her writings, don't hesitate to get in touch with her on LinkedIn to start a conversation. You can also find her on https://medium.com.

Printed in the USA
CPSIA information can be obtained
at www.ICGtesting.com
LVHW062048250524
781397LV00012B/114

9 798891 5791